Finding Your Superhorse

8 Keys to Developing the Horse That's Just Right for You

— LYNN PALM —

with *Rebecca M. Didier* and *Marie-Frances Davis*

Forewords by *Stephanie Lynn, Carla Wennberg, Kevin Dukes* and *Paola Donarini*

Trafalgar Square
North Pomfret, Vermont

First published in 2023 by
Trafalgar Square Books
North Pomfret, Vermont 05053

Copyright © 2023 *Lynn Palm*

All rights reserved. No part of this book may be reproduced, by any means, without written permission of the publisher, except by a reviewer quoting brief excerpts for a review in a magazine, newspaper, or website.

Disclaimer of Liability
The authors and publisher shall have neither liability nor responsibility to any person or entity with respect to any loss or damage caused or alleged to be caused directly or indirectly by the information contained in this book. While the book is as accurate as the authors can make it, there may be errors, omissions, and inaccuracies.

Trafalgar Square Books encourages the use of approved safety helmets in all equestrian sports and activities.

Library of Congress Cataloging-in-Publication Data
Names: Palm, Lynn, author. | Didier, Rebecca, 1977- author. | Davis, Marie-Frances, author.
Title: Finding your superhorse : 8 keys to developing the horse that's just right for you / Lynn Palm with Rebecca Didier and Marie-Frances Davis.
Description: North Pomfret, Vermont : Trafalgar Square Books, 2023. | Summary: "For six decades, Lynn Palm has been a mainstay of the horse training, showing, and clinicing industry. Her successes in diversity in training and the development of willingness and ability across disciplines are unparalleled. She has four Superhorse Titles-a prize awarded to a horse that demonstrates a broad skillset and proficiency in multiple sports. In these pages, Lynn shares the eight keys to her success in training and competing, and how you, too-whether you're eventing or ranch riding-can shape a horse with a good attitude, correct movement, healthy biomechanics, and top-notch conditioning. A "Superhorse" will take you farther for longer, and you'll enjoy every minute of it"-- Provided by publisher.
Identifiers: LCCN 2023001051 (print) | LCCN 2023001052 (ebook) | ISBN 9781646011339 (paperback) | ISBN 9781646011346 (epub)
Subjects: LCSH: Horses--Training. | Horsemanship.
Classification: LCC SF287 .P348 2023 (print) | LCC SF287 (ebook) | DDC 636.1/0835--dc23/eng/20230512
LC record available at https://lccn.loc.gov/2023001051
LC ebook record available at https://lccn.loc.gov/2023001052

All photographs by Cappy Jackson *except*: I.1, I.2, 1.5, 2.1, 2.9 A & B, 2.10, 3.1, 3.4, 3.5, 3.6 A & B, 4.2 A & B, 5.4, 6.1 A & B, 6.2, 6.4, 6.6, 7.1, 7.5, 8.1, C.1 (Courtesy of Palm Equestrian Academy); I.3 (Don Trout); 1.1, 1.2, 1.4, 7.3 (Betty Salvatori); 1.3 (*LIFE Magazine*); 2.2 (Tracy Thompson); 3.7 (Waltenberry); 3.8 (Breyer); 3.9 (*Paint Horse Journal*); 3.10 (Daniel DeWeese); 3.14 A & B (Erin Winkowski); 4.8, 5.2, 8.3 (Photos by Furey); 5.1 A & B (Sarah Gentry); 5.3 (Larry Williams); 5.6 (Cyril Pittion-Rossillon); 6.5 (Debbie Fitzgerald); 7.4 (Shane Rux Photography); 8.5 (Chris Hamilton); C.2 (Rich Tewell)

An effort has been made to contact all photographers who could be identified. In some cases a photographer may not have been found. Should additional photographers be identified, they will be credited in future editions.

Illustrations and book design by *Katarzyna Misiukanis–Celińska (https://misiukanis-artstudio.com)*
Cover design by *RM Didier*
Typefaces: *Adobe Text Pro, Fino Sans, Lato, Playfair Display* and *Sloop*
Index by *Andrea M. Jones (www.jonesliteraryservice.com)*

Printed in China
10 9 8 7 6 5 4 3 2 1

— DEDICATION —

*I would like
to dedicate this to my family
for being my best mentors
and cheerleaders.*

I am so grateful to have had parents like mine. My dad was an entrepreneur in the contact lens manufacturing business, holding two patents with soft lenses. He was always teaching and focused to succeed. My mom was the rock of the family who knew how to support her kids even if she did not know anything about their interests—she would learn about it. She was always involved in arts, crafts, sewing, cooking, clubs—just an everything Mom. She was the social butterfly that I am today!

To my late brother, Phillip. He was an amazingly talented modern ballet dancer who was lucky enough to dance all over the world. The Martha Graham Dance Company recognized his talents and took them to new levels. I will never forget the night I got to watch him perform at the Metropolitan Opera House in New York City as he danced a solo performance with Liza Minnelli narrating *The Owl and the Pussy Cat* by Edward Lear. His aspirations as a dancer inspired me to reach for the stars!

This goes to my best friend and husband, Cyril Pittion-Rossillon. Since first meeting in Ocala in 1989, we were attracted to each other because of trying to do our best with horses. We married two years later. Cyril has been the best supporter of me and my horses for competition as well my exhibitions with Rugged Lark. We were the best team together, winning the AQHA Superhorse Title with The Lark Ascending! Cyril has also been a mentor to me in how to teach equestrian sport for multiple disciplines. Our dressage backgrounds are very similar in that we train and teach with classical principles to bring out the best in horses with lightness. As a graduate of the French National Riding School, his wealth of knowledge and experience has given me so much for my own teaching. I have become better by listening and watching his success teaching riders to "become the riders their horses deserve."

to Rugged Lark

My "boyfriend" of 16 years in training, competing, and performing. We had such a great relationship and understanding. We loved to travel, compete, entertain, go to cocktail parties, and do TV shows! Lark just loved people and to perform. He made so many offspring with the same great attitude to perform their best, whether in the show arena or out riding the country or pulling a sleigh. He was a horse of a lifetime. The first AQHA World Champion Superhorse and the only sire to sire two Superhorse offspring—The Lark Ascending and Look Whos Larkin—Rugged Lark was *truly* my Superhorse and my "horse of a lifetime"!

and to Rugged Painted Lark

One of my many "super horses," he was one of several who followed his father's footsteps. We called him "Bruce" after the handsome Bruce Willis, and he was such a special horse that had not only to be a "hero" for his sire Rugged Lark and his brother My Royal Lark, he also loved to perform to the song *Hero* by Mariah Carey. He learned in such a short time to perform many advance movements without a bridle and to jump and do some tricks for entertainment, as well. He loved to do it all, as he was a showoff. He was most known in the educational arena, providing demonstrations of dressage principles for Western types of horses. Our highlights were performing at the FEI World Equestrian Games in 2010 in Kentucky and the FEI World Cup in 2017 in Omaha, Nebraska. Rugged Painted Lark was the first horse in a Western saddle in an FEI dressage and jumping arena, introducing Western dressage in the United States. He loved the audience. The louder the audience, the better he would perform!

FOUR FOREWORDS
Stephanie Lynn – VIII
Carla Wennberg – VIII
Kevin Dukes – X
Paola Donarini – XI

INTRODUCTION
Horsemanship Is a Lifelong Quest
– 1 –

"Enjoy the journey."

CHAPTER 1
Modest Beginnings Can Be the Foundation of Something Great
– 9 –

"Opportunities don't happen, you create them."
– Chris Grosser, Entrepreneur –

CHAPTER 2
Groundwork Makes the Dream Work
– 27 –

"If your horse is well-mannered and obedient on the ground, you are building the rapport you need in the saddle."
– Carol Harris –

CHAPTER 3
Patience Now Pays Off Later
– 65 –

"The longer you take to train the horse, the longer you will have with him."
– Bobbi Steele –

CHAPTER 4
There's No Better Mirror of Our Insides or Outsides
– 113 –

"The better you ride, the better your horse goes."

CHAPTER 5
THE COMPETITIVE EDGE SERVES YOU WELL, EVEN IF YOU NEVER SHOW
– 143 –

"Success is made of a thousand failures."

CHAPTER 6
OPTIMISM AND ETHICS ARE THE KEYS TO SUCCESS
– 163 –

"It will be alright. Things will work out okay."
– Heidi Burkhalter –

CHAPTER 7
NEVER FORGET: THEY JUST WANT TO EAT GRASS ALL DAY
– 191 –

"Horses don't have a choice."

CHAPTER 8
OUR HORSES PAY IT FORWARD AND GIVE BACK. WE SHOULD, TOO.
– 217 –

"When with your horse, remind yourself you're lovin' life!"

CONCLUSION
IN THE END, IT'S REALLY ABOUT WHAT YOU CAN DO ON YOUR OWN TIME WITH YOUR OWN HORSE
– 241 –

"Not all knowledge is good knowledge.
I'd rather have useful knowledge."

ACKNOWLEDGMENTS
– 248 –

INDEX
– 249 –

FOUR
FOREWORDS

Stephanie Lynn
Carla Wennberg

Kevin Dukes
Paola Donarini

Lynn Palm is a master horseman. As the title of her new book alludes, good communication between horse and rider builds not only a Superhorse, but also a superior horseman. Lynn's ability to communicate with horses exceeds that of most equestrians. It is second only to her gift to share this knowledge in a meaningful way, improving aspiring riders as they chart their course to building happy, healthy horses.

Lynn's instruction continues to shape countless journeys for riders of various disciplines across the globe. In this new book, you will get to hear about the special people who helped Lynn become the master she is today. You will also find many anecdotal lessons of life in the barn as it mirrors life outside of the barn.

Enjoy the book, soak in the words, and as she told me decades ago while under her employ, "Stop, take a breath, and think like a horse."

Have fun reading. And I highly recommend you follow her advice. It will bring a lifetime of contentedness, on and off the horse.

– **STEPHANIE LYNN** –
NSBA Executive Director
Former AQHA, NSBA, and APHA Judge,
Author, World Champion, and Coach

I am honored to write a few words to appear in Lynn Palm's book Finding Your Superhorse, as Lynn has been in my life for over 50 years because of horses! Lynn has been a mentor to me, which started when I purchased my first registered Quarter Horse. As a horse trainer and coach, she instilled not only correct training of the horse, but more importantly, that the horse comes first. Welfare of the horse has always been foremost to Lynn, and I so appreciate that I learned from her early in my career to make it a priority. Her entire career, so much as I have experienced it, has been welfare-focused through the correct training of the horse—not what seems to be a trend.

I enjoyed great success as a young rider, when Lynn contributed to many important lessons learned, always exhibiting amazing professionalism in lessons and the training of my horses. She even gave me her personal horse for a summer to learn on—her mare Mocha Dell, who was a great teacher to me and would bow on command! How cool is that for a 4-H and Quarter Horse kid? Of course, I grew up and became a professional myself, and I am now so thankful to Lynn for giving me such a great start.

I have seen Lynn show many AQHA World Champions and Superhorse winners. I watched her perform at the 1996 Olympics in Atlanta on the stallion Rugged Lark—there, in the Olympic dressage arena, they not only demonstrated his dressage training, but also jumped a fence and spun like a reiner, showing off the immense versatility of that amazing horse! I have experienced many times Lynn showing the versatility of the American Quarter Horse, in many different kinds of classes, but I have also had the pleasure of watching her compete in both traditional dressage as well as Western dressage, which inspired my own love for it. In fact, I have my USDF bronze and silver medals in traditional dressage, and also because of Lynn, I now have a Quarter Horse showing in Western dressage competitions!

Lynn and I have also shared over 30 years of AQHA judging experiences. I love the many discussions we have had about many different events and how we can represent our sports better in judging correctness. Lynn is a true visionary, and she has never been afraid to speak up and promote great ideas for the future of our horse industry.

Dedication is the best word I could choose to describe Lynn. As a horseman, I have never met a better trainer. As a coach, she has an incredible background, with a true eye to help you become a partner with your horse. She is a winner, and she knows how to produce a winner.

As a longtime mentor to me on my journey in the horse industry, I also love and appreciate her as a friend. I'm so very thankful to have her in my life.

– **Carla Wennberg** –
Instructor and Coach St. Andrews University in N.C.
AQHA/NSBA judge
AQHA Professional Horseman
IHSA Lifetime Achievement Award
AQHA Judges Committee Member

I am so excited that Lynn Palm has decided to share her incredible knowledge with the public in this inspiring book, *Finding Your Superhorse*. As one of my mentors, Lynn shared her knowledge with me. And if it weren't for that knowledge, I wouldn't be where I am today.

I've had a very successful career with over 35 world championships in eight different events across multiple breeds. I owe a huge part of my success to Lynn and her willingness to mentor me. Her teachings have been and are the foundation of my own training program today.

Lynn continues to raise the bar and strive for perfection—but never at the expense of the horse. I truly believe the most important lesson she taught me is to keep "L.A.R.K" in your training program: *Love, Acceptance, Respect, and Kindness.* Lynn is one of the greatest horsepeople of our time. Please read this book, follow her lead, and you will always have success.

– KEVIN DUKES –
Dukes Performance Horses
Weatherford, Texas

IN the mid-1980s, I was searching through the *The American Quarter Horse Journal* and found an advertisement for Lynn Palm at the Royal Palm Ranch in Bessemer, Michigan. I knew this was a long way from Italy, but I was intrigued by her all-around horse training. I wanted to go to the United States and train with Lynn Palm. I wrote a letter to Lynn, and she responded, and we made a plan to meet.

My adventure really began at the 1986 AQHA World Championship Show. I met Lynn for the first time just as she was winning both World and Reserve World Championships in Junior Trail. It was thrilling! I was excited to then travel with her to Michigan and spend time learning from her. Imagine my excitement when the first horse she put me on was Rugged Lark! I knew if I did not ride him very well (which I didn't), I had a big problem.

From there, Lynn became my mentor, and I took her every word, knowing that what she was teaching me would make me a better rider. And so it did. Every year for more than ten years following my first visit, she came and taught clinics for us in Italy and helped me with my horses via long-distance instruction. We always stayed in touch and continue to do so today as both colleagues and friends.

Lynn is very special in many ways. Most of all, she is generous with her time and knowledge. She is determined to make all riders better for their horses, and she inspires many others to do the same, myself included.

My success in Italy with horses, training, and competition comes from all that Lynn has given me for so many years. She made an imprint on me that is as strong today as the first time I met her. We have so many great memories, and I feel she is always on my shoulder. This book puts her on your shoulder, too.

– PAOLA DONARINI –
ALBA Quarter Horses 3.0
Siena, Italy

— INTRODUCTION —

HORSEMANSHIP IS A LIFELONG QUEST

"Enjoy the journey."

Since 1978, the title of "Superhorse" has been the most prestigious award at the American Quarter Horse Association (AQHA) World Championships Show.

"Superhorse is the ironman, or ironhorse," says the AQHA. The title is presented to the horse that earns the most points in three or more events at the show.

It's a prize that is meant to show diversity in training, to demonstrate willingness and ability across disciplines. It's intended to recognize that the sky's the limit when it comes to our great American breed, the Quarter Horse. English, Western, jumping, roping, driving, ranch riding, dressage—you name it, these horses can do it. That's part of the reason why I've been riding, training, and showing Quarter Horses for six decades. There's so much fun and potential in every ride.

Only a handful of horses have won the title of Superhorse multiple times, and one of them is Rugged Lark, the remarkable stallion bred by Teresa Streigel and owned by Carol Harris that I had the honor of showing the years he won: 1985 and 1987. Only a few people have shown multiple horses to Superhorse titles—I got the chance on three: Skip's Sierra Nick in 1981, Rugged Lark in his two years, and then his son, The Lark Ascending, in 1991. These titles brought press, media attention, sponsorships. The horses were invited to appear at special events as "equine celebrities." For sure, the Superhorse titles impacted my career. And to some, maybe, the horses who won seemed singular in their varied abilities.

The thing is, though, I believe we can all have a Superhorse of our own—the horse that does it all, and does it willingly and with style. It doesn't matter which breed you prefer or whether you're eventing or ranch riding—a horse with a good attitude, correct movement, healthy biomechanics, and conscientious conditioning will take you farther for longer, and you'll enjoy every minute of it.

Sounds pretty good, right? I can help you achieve this. I want to help you achieve this. That is why I wrote this book. All these years and all these adventures with horses and all these experiences teaching others—there's loads here that can make your Superhorse dreams reality. In the eight chapters ahead, I'll share what I think are eight "keys" or ideas to help guide you in your horsemanship journey, as well as stories of moments that taught me valuable lessons on mine. In addition, I provide a few of my very favorite exercises—the ones I rely on to regularly bring horses along and successfully compete them. These days, my focus is dressage and Western dressage, and there's nothing more cross-disciplinary and necessary to a horse's development and longevity, in my mind. If there is one thing I hope to convince you in these pages, it is the value of basic dressage training for all horses, regardless of their "jobs" or activities.

I.1 • All my Superhorses competed in Pleasure Driving, including my 1981 winner Skip's Sierra Nick.

I.2 • The Lark Ascending ("Larkie") was a striking horse to look at, and that is one reason I bought him at the All American Quarter Horse Congress in 1989. I sold him to a pair of sisters, Janet Reid and Ethel Strach, before competing for the Superhorse title, and winning, in 1991.

> "I NEVER DREAMED ABOUT SUCCESS.
> I WORKED FOR IT."
>
> – Estée Lauder –
> Beauty Business Entrepreneur

I.3 A & B • Rugged Lark won the title of Superhorse twice, in 1985 and 1987, and he was the sire of two more Superhorses. What a special stallion, and I am honored to have been his partner and friend for so many years.

I came from a modest home and was not of "horsey" blood. But I'm of an era when hard work and commitment could change your stars. I benefited from wonderful mentors—some of whom I will tell you about so you can learn from them, too—but I would never have gotten to where I am today without grit and a real desire to evolve as a horsewoman. It isn't unusual to hear people say that one of the things they like best about riding and training is that you're always learning. This isn't a static career, one where you reach the top of a mountain and look at a view and think, "There, I've done it!" The goal posts are always moving, because you can always learn more and do better, not just for ribbons and prize money, but for the horses themselves.

Horsemanship is a lifelong quest, one that I am still on. And that is what is most rewarding.

INTRODUCTION 7

— CHAPTER 1 —

MODEST BEGINNINGS CAN BE THE FOUNDATION FOR SOMETHING GREAT

> *"Opportunities don't happen,
> you create them."*
>
> – Chris Grosser –
> Entrepreneur

A Sweet Start

It isn't an unusual place to begin for a horse girl, the story where I finally talked my parents into getting me a pony. My mom always said that as soon as I could stand, I used the window ledge to hold me up as I looked outside for our neighbor's black-and-white pony, named Sweet Honor. I looked for her every day! But it wasn't until quite a few years later that my dad and I went to Cain's Pony Farm outside Sarasota, Florida. I had always admired the farm when we passed it in the car—its board fences and ponies of all colors dotting the pastures as far as I could see. To actually turn down the driveway with Dad, knowing I was really getting a pony, was the most exciting moment of my young life. Together, he and I looked at all the available sale ponies. I kept going back to a sweet bay with the biggest brown eyes, like a deer. Dad was against my choice, as we were told the pony was pregnant! He was wiser than he knew, trying to steer clear, but I somehow convinced him this pregnant pony was the perfect first horse for our family.

I named the bay pony Sugar, and it wasn't too long after she came home that Sugar had Honey, a beautiful dark-colored filly with a flaxen mane and tail. I was in heaven! Not only did I have one pony—I now had two. They were my best friends, and I spent every moment I could with them.

But we knew nothing about keeping horses or raising foals. When we started out, Sugar was tied out on a rope in our yard. We thought she would be just fine living on Florida grass....

We'd moved to Sarasota when I was seven. A lady with horses lived down the street, and I would ride my bike over to watch her ride. One day she introduced herself: her name was Bobbi Steele, and she would become my mentor. I rode with her for over 30 years, and my parents never paid for one lesson.

It was Ms. Steele, along with my mom, who got me into 4-H, which saved us and our ponies! 4-H was and is one of the largest youth development organizations in the United States. It is supported by a community of more than 100 public universities and hundreds of thousands of volunteers, and provides experiences where young people "learn by doing" in areas that interest them—like caring for and showing animals. 4-H helped me learn the basic equine management skills I needed to have two ponies at home.

Ultimately, I succeeded in training Sugar to be a driving pony and did sulky races with her. I rode Honey and taught her to perform tricks. She was the fastest pony in the neighborhood and was the best partner when we played hide-and-seek in the orange groves with my friends because she was very responsive to my leg cues and reins. Those games with the neighbor kids were epic: bareback, barefoot, no helmet...life was at its best!

A (Really) Good Neighbor

My curiosity and love for horses had drawn me to Ms. Steele's place down the street, and the day she introduced herself would not only change my ponies' lives, it would change mine.

1.1 • Sugar was my first pony...and she made Honey!

1.2 • I practiced everything I learned with Ms. Steele with my ponies. Honey learned tricks, like sitting, which I still like to incorporate in my training with horses today to add variety and fun.

1.3 • In 1946, *Life Magazine* featured a story about my mentor Ms. Bobbi Steele and included photos of the dressage movements and tricks she performed in her popular exhibitions. This is a scan from the copy I still have!

1.4 • Ms. Bobbi Steele taught me to appreciate all disciplines and what each can bring to the training of the horse and the rider. Here she clears a nearly 6-foot fence!

Ms. Steele's story was a unique one. She'd been born on a farm in Illinois, but her parents wouldn't let her have a horse, so as a teenager, she had literally "run away and joined the circus." Ringling Brothers hired her as a rider, and because they employed European horse trainers for their equestrian acts, Ms. Steele would spend the next 10 years under the guidance of German dressage master Captain William Hyer, becoming one of the first women in the United States to ride dressage. She and the exhibition horses she trained would gain fame as performers, earning her a feature story in a 1946 issue of *LIFE Magazine.*

Ms. Steele told me that if I wanted a horse, I had to become a good rider. She insisted on the importance of this, whatever it was that I eventually wanted to do with horses. The better a rider I became, the more I would be able to achieve with them. Ms. Steele met and worked with many riders, but she recognized in me a natural talent for both riding and understanding horses. She knew that I was passionate; I worked very, very hard on anything that she took the time to teach me, and always asked questions to learn more. *She* understood horses and took it upon herself to teach *me* how. All breeds, and all conformation, form to function, fascinated me. Ms. Steele taught me how a horse looked and moved when performing

KEEPING STRAIGHTNESS AND CROOKEDNESS STRAIGHT

All horses are naturally crooked, as they have a "soft" or "easy" side and a "stiff" or "harder" side. Usually, the left side of the horse is the horse's soft side, as traditionally we do most of our handling from this side. The right side is the stiff side. We have to develop horses to have two soft sides, both left and right. When we don't, they will "fall out" or lean to the right when traveling to the left (especially on a circle), and they will "fall in" or lean inward when going to the right. When this happens with the horse's balance, we say he is "crooked," and not "straight."

When traveling on a straight line, the horse's body follows his head. If you don't keep his body straight with leg aids and guidance from the reins, you will have a very "wiggly" straight line—again, your horse is "crooked" not "straight." In transitions, if you do not control the horse's soft and stiff sides, he may move left or right with both his body and head, thus being "crooked" (and you will have a poor, delayed transition).

You can tell when a horse is "straight" on either a straight or curving line (such as a circle) when the horse's hind legs are tracking exactly in the line of the front legs—right hind to right front, left hind to left front. When the horse is "straight" in his body alignment, he achieves balance and self-carriage (when the horse can maintain his frame and rhythm on his own, without relying on the rider's aids).

in correct balance. She showed me what it took to train a horse with understanding and the best ways to communicate with the horse for him to understand what we are asking. She taught me how to recognize the horse's personality, and his instincts and behaviors. Every day I spent with her, Ms. Steele taught me more about "how to read a horse."

Ms. Steele had a three-year-old Saddlebred/Quarter Horse cross named Nic Nack—a beautiful red chestnut with a blaze and four perfect stockings to his knees and hocks. Well-built and short-coupled with a neck that tied in perfectly to his sloping shoulder and a beautiful head, Nic Nack looked like his name suggested: a perfect toy horse you would want to buy in a store. He was a cribber, though, and that habit drove Ms. Steele nuts! She was always fixing fence and painting boards with something to try and keep him from chewing them. I just thought he was so smart that he knew how to get you to come out of the house to fix or paint something!

Nic Nack would be the horse that became the foundation of my training as a rider. Ms. Steele was starting him on the ground and under saddle, and recognizing my natural passion for horses and hunger to learn, she let me ride him. I clearly remember one summer, Ms. Steele worked with me six days a week, just sitting-trot circles to learn how to collect Nic Nack's body from my seat and legs with guidance from my hands. I was determined to succeed with these "boring" exercises in order to achieve a horse that was "collected," "on the bit," and "connected"—words I'd heard from Ms. Steele and knew were meaningful when it came to horsemanship.

Ms. Steele's patient work with me on Nic Nack's straightness and balance—and shaping our ability to ride a perfect round circle—is how I learned to collect a horse in the ways necessary for higher levels of training. I learned that to keep the horse on a round circle in each direction, the rider had to create bend in the horse through the leg aids first, as the leg aids controlled the majority of the horse's body—from the withers to the dock of the tail. The rein aids (the rider's hands) guided the forehand—from the withers to the horse's poll. The leg aids kept the horse "straight" on the curving line. (I know this sounds like it can't be possible, but it is. I explain more

1.5 • Riding Ms. Steele's horse Nic Nack at a 4-H Open Show in 1967 in Sarasota, Florida.

"INSIDE," "OUTSIDE"

There can be confusion when the terms "inside" and "outside" are used in relation to the horse. These terms have nothing to do with the horse's position in an arena but instead indicate the horse's direction of flexion or bend. Picture the horse on a curving line, with his body bent in the shape of a banana. The horse is flexed to the "inside" of this bend so you can just see his eye on the side of the "inside" rein. The horse's muscles on the "inside" have to compress.

The "outside" of the horse's body ("outside" of the bend) has to stretch on the curving line. The "outside" rein keeps the horse's body alignment and connects the horse back to front (hindquarters to forehand). The rider's "outside" leg supports straightness in the horse and encourages the horse's body to bend around the rider's "inside" leg, thus controlling the horse's body alignment and balance.

about it in the sidebar on p. 16.) They make sure he does not "fall in" or "fall out" on the circle.

The hands, meanwhile, kept the horse's front legs on the curved path, with his head flexed inward slightly, just enough to see the "inside" eye of the horse, and the "outside" rein ensuring the horse remained in alignment—the "outside" rein was what connected the horse from poll to tail.

For a whole summer vacation, six days a week, I worked some part of my lesson with Ms. Steele on just these sitting-trot circles!

During the lesson, Ms. Steele always found a positive in the ride, recognizing what I had managed to achieve consistently, instead of just acknowledging short moments of success. She continued to explain why what we were doing with the circle exercise was going to develop Nic Nack to be more connected, thus allowing me to both lengthen and collect his gaits, incorporate more difficult transitions, and eventually be capable of advanced lateral work, canter pirouettes, tempi changes, and even passage and piaffe.

I couldn't wait to learn it all!

I rode Nic Nack for six years before she let us go off the property to show off our training. When

we proved to her that we could show flowing and correct trot half-pass, canter half-pass, flying lead changes (including tempi changes), canter pirouettes, and some fun tricks, she let me take him to local shows and "wow" everyone. I remember how beautiful and "buff" Nic Nack was by then from all our careful training. Ms. Steele even let me take him to North Carolina to perform a dressage routine at the State 4-H Horse Show Finals, which was a big deal for her. It all went well, and we were very proud of what we had accomplished together.

The best part of every lesson with Ms. Steele was after we were done and had taken care of Nic Nack, we would go inside her house and sit down, each with a small glass bottle of Coke, and talk about what we'd done that day. She would explain the "why" and what stage of training was next, how what we were doing now was getting Nic Nack ready for what we might want him to do in the future. She always related her commonsense techniques and exercises to the idea of, "How would you feel?"—as if I was the horse. This idea of considering the horse's perspective and the same classical dressage fundamentals Ms. Steele helped me learn on Nic Nack are still what I use today with all my own horses and students. With Ms. Steele, I was learning more than how to ride, build my skills, and train a young horse to his most advanced capabilities. She was also teaching me how to *teach*.

My First "Superhorses"

If I look back now at what I did with Sugar and Honey and Nic Nack, I can see how I was already cultivating a desire for the "all-arounder" with an excellent foundation and conditioning that would allow him to do anything. It wasn't about a particular discipline—yes, I was learning dressage in Bobbi Steele's riding ring, but what we were doing wasn't the end goal. The end goal was to develop Nic Nack's physique and responsiveness so he was not just beautiful, but a pleasure to ride, whatever we did. Everything I learned with Ms. Steele I took home and practiced with my own ponies, and they, too, only became fitter and more enjoyable with the training.

Nic Nack was a grade cross. Sugar and Honey were ponies plucked from a field by a child with little experience or knowledge. And yet, all three became exactly what they needed to be—sound, capable, and willing performers in multiple disciplines. Take a good look at the horse you have in your barn. I promise you that with consistent use of basic dressage, he too can look and ride like a Superhorse. Fancy bloodlines are not required! If you have them, you still need to put in the time to enable your horse to live up to all that his papers promise. This is the great leveling of the horse world: potential greatness is in every paddock and every stall, if only we are willing to do our part in the partnership.

And this potential applies to us, as well. As I mentioned earlier, I came from very modest beginnings—my family wasn't "horsey," and we didn't have money. And yet, because of the opportunities that 4-H provided and my willingness to work hard under Bobbi Steele's experienced eye, I could develop into a strong, balanced, sophisticated rider with an understanding for the horse and what proper training could do for him. I did have the good luck of having Ms. Steele as a willing mentor and neighbor, but knowledge and guidance are actually far more available now than when I was a child.

1.7 • Hot N Royal showing a really nice relaxed, uphill balance for a Western horse. This ideal outline can be achieved with practice on the collected circle, both in and outside the arena.

With the internet, more and more of us have access to the training techniques of professionals from around the world. There are literally thousands of ways at our fingertips to educate ourselves and grow and improve—if we are willing to put in the time and effort.

My Favorite Exercise to Improve Yourself and Improve Your Horse

Collection on a Circle with Transitions

This exercise was one that Ms. Steele and I did the most in order to develop the horse's ability to collect and compact his body in a more uphill balance, thus distributing more weight to the hind legs. It would be so nice if you used your aids once and your horse just stayed on the circle. But let me tell you, this does not happen! For you to have a consistent round circle and control the same tempo in the gait, you must manage the horse *every stride*. This must be accomplished first by riding a round 20-meter circle and keeping the same tempo in all gaits before you can aim for collection.

Collection is achieved by developing the horse to keep the *bend* and *straightness*, thus *balance*, through many transitions on the circle and doing 15-meter, 10-meter, and 8-meter circles. These upward and downward transitions and smaller circles encourage *engagement* of the horse's hind legs, where they bear more weight, thus building power from behind. They also develop an uphill balance, allowing the horse to raise and round his back, and lighten his forehand—his poll comes up and his neck rounds, compacting the horse's body. This is what we call *collection*. Developing correct collection takes years, and when you get it, it is amazing how athletic, agile, and light a horse gets in his self-carriage and performance.

Start by riding a 20-meter circle to the left, and aim to ride a *truly* round circle. This is *not* easy! To keep the circle round you must manage the body

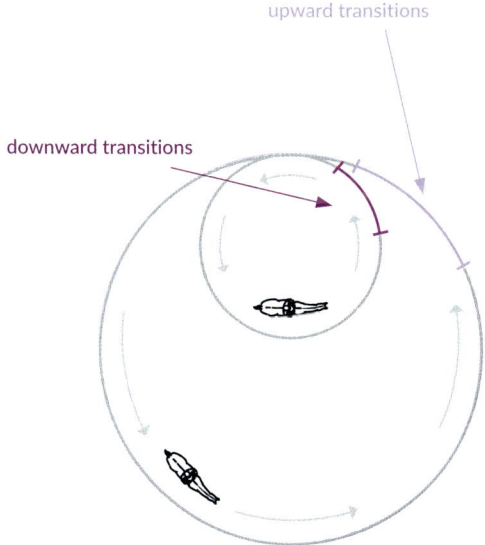

position of your horse, keeping him bending and straight on the circle at all times. Here's how:

★ Your left opening or neck rein flexes the horse's head to the left (the inside).

★ Your left (inside) leg aid at the girth asks the horse to bend his body at the rib cage.

★ The right (outside) rein keeps the horse straight and does not let the neck bend too far to the inside. The outside rein also keeps the horse's body aligned and straight, so the right hind leg tracks to the right front, and left hind leg tracks to the left front.

★ The right (outside) leg aid keeps the horse's hips from swinging out and maintains the alignment and straightness on the curving line to the left.

1.6 • Once your 20-meter circle is active in the gaits and straight, you can progress to smaller circles, which require better balance and more engagement from your horse.

POSITIVE INFLUENCERS

– Martha Josey –

I grew to admire legendary barrel racer and Rodeo Hall of Fame Inductee Martha Josey because of her educational programs and the competitions she developed for kids. Her clinics were the first in her sport, and she has taught thousands of riders over the years.

I will never forget watching Martha ride a beautiful Palomino down to the ring at our Women LUV Horses event in North Carolina (see p. 219). I asked her about the horse and she explained that she was schooling him to be quiet and walk at new venues, as he usually got very excited. She went on to say that she trained a lot of time at the walk. "If you spend the time to get your horse to think slow, he will run faster on the barrels." It reminded me of Ms. Steele telling me that you couldn't train a horse or get a maximum performance from a horse if he was "thinking fast." I've always remembered since then that when "you get your horse to think slow, he will run faster."

★ Put your weight "down" in the saddle, sitting centered, with your weight distributed equally. (Know that your balance will feel naturally pulled to the outside because of the sensation of centrifugal force, but on a 20-meter circle, you want your weight in your seat bones to be even.) Make sure your shoulders stay back in a vertical position over your hips. When you put weight on the horse's back in this way, you are giving him the incentive and encouragement to engage the inside hind leg deeper under the barrel. Any time the horse slows down, gets a little "flat," or wants to fall in or out with his body, *sit* more. I recently attended a clinic with British Olympian Carl Hester, which I enjoyed very much, and he told every rider, even those already riding Grand Prix, "Sit!" (with a particular emphasis on that ending "t")! He didn't want stronger legs and he didn't want stronger hands—he wanted the riders to *sit*.

★ Repeat in a circle to the right.

★ When the circle is round, straight, and forward at 20 meters in both directions, advance to a circle of 15 meters, and then to 10 meters. The smaller the circles get, the harder it is to control the horse's balance. He will lose his balance by falling in and falling out. You need more engagement from behind (the hind legs stepping farther underneath the horse's

> "IF YOU THINK YOU KNOW
> EVERYTHING ABOUT HORSES,
> YOU'LL ALWAYS STAY AT ONE LEVEL."
>
> – Bobbi Steele –

body) and more power from the horse to propel him around that smaller circle, so you do have to sit more to engage the hind end more, and with the smaller circle, your weight moves slightly to the outside.

When your horse accepts your leg, seat, and rein aids and grows stronger in his body through progressive conditioning, he will do the circle task with ease and willingness. This means you have achieved balance in your horse, which will make it easier for him to complete difficult transitions, maintain tempo in all gaits, connect his hind legs to your hands, and develop the self-carriage necessary to collect. Ms. Steele always told me that too few people were willing to spend the time we were spending on the circle exercise, every ride after our warm-up. With the tiniest progression, she assured me that we were succeeding—and you can, too!

— CHAPTER 2 —

GROUNDWORK MAKES THE DREAM WORK

> *"If your horse is well-mannered and obedient on the ground, you are building the rapport you need in the saddle."*
>
> – Carol Harris –

Through my involvement with 4-H as a youth, I learned a lot about important aspects of horse care and training. For example, there is a class at most 4-H shows called "Fitting and Showmanship." The purpose of this class, according to official 4-H materials, is to "encourage members to maintain high standards for horse management and responsibility to their 4-H project animals." It is meant to provide a way to measure and reward participants for learning to properly care for their horses and show them to their "best advantage."

Fitting and Showmanship was always a required class when I was in 4-H. I so appreciate that now, looking back, as it taught us safe and controlled handling of our horses on the ground. I did well, but it actually was not one of my best events as a young competitor. Why? I always had kind of "lazy" horses, and the best Showmanship horses are highly sensitive and aware, yet sensible.

In this class, competitors had to enter the ring in an order, and I learned to always try to be in the first three because my horse had the tendency to fall asleep while waiting, and then I would have a sluggish first part of the

pattern we had to perform in hand for the judge. I will never forget one year at the 4-H State Show in Florida, I found myself way back in line—about twenty-fifth to go—and my horse Mocha Dell and I had to stand and wait in the warm morning sun. Of course, she went to sleep. However, I waited until there were only two horses left before we were up, then gave her a few small carrot pieces. She woke up just in time! When it was our turn, we had a good performance, and while we did not win, we did place high.

Essential Preparation

Showing a horse in hand, as you do in Fitting and Showmanship, requires as much practice and preparation as showing in a riding class. So my commitment to groundwork began pretty early, as I was a competitive person and wanted to do well. Later, as my skills and understanding developed, I found groundwork—in-hand exercises, longeing, long-lining—an essential step in any horse's development. In our barn, it is done with all our horses. With young stock, groundwork is a must to make an easy progression to under-saddle work. It allows me to keep the horse confident while providing a great introduction to what you need him to learn about the leg and rein aids under saddle. With older or more experienced horses, groundwork allows me to learn more about them before I work them under saddle, and it is also valuable when settling in at a horse show.

Good groundwork training puts you on the path to having a Superhorse. Rugged Lark is a great example of this: I worked him in hand, longed, and long-lined him. Then, when I decided to teach him to pull a cart, he proved to me the value of all his previous lessons. Lark was so confident and had such trust in our partnership, I had him pulling the cart in one lesson! That is not something people can do with most horses.

A Sensible Groundwork Program

There are six different components to the groundwork program I use:

2.1 • Sun' Gold Ray was my second registered Quarter Horse. Here we are competing in a Showmanship class.

★ **1. IN-HAND WORK:** This is about manners on the ground. Working on leading politely at the walk and trot, halting, backing up (first straight, and when this is done well, on curving lines in each direction), squaring the legs, standing without being tied (ground-tying), pivots in both directions—I like to begin with all the basic skills I had to learn in 4-H for the required Showmanship classes.

When the horse is ready, I also school basic lateral work in-hand: turn-on-the-forehand, yielding (preparation for leg-yield—see p. 211), and turn-on-the-haunches. Mastering these movements on the ground first improves your chances of success when you later ask for them under saddle.

★ **2. WORKING AT LIBERTY:** All groundwork techniques teach a handler about her horse, as well as improving the horse's concentration and response on command. Liberty work (and longeing, too, which I discuss next—p. 35) is wonderful for exercise and fitness. However, it is most important as a way to learn your horse's natural self-carriage. You can then evaluate his athleticism and determine what he is best suited to do and what kind of timeline he might need to accomplish that.

Liberty is often how I will first evaluate a horse and his movement, and also how I continue to check in and assess his development as he becomes more athletic and moves with more fluidity and relaxation.

It is another way you can keep working on the horse's strength, balance, and self-carriage without riding him. Training the horse without the weight of the rider adds variety, reduces load-bearing, and gives you an opportunity to evaluate your horse from the ground as he learns to concentrate and respond correctly to your commands.

Liberty brings together what you teach the horse in-hand and what you will be working with on the longe line: your position on the ground, your whip used properly as an extension of your arm to encourage the horse to go forward, and the correct tone of voice to request and reward are all practiced. You must be parallel to the horse and keep him moving forward and balanced and not falling in or out. It is important that you do

2.2 • I am leading My Royal Lark ("Wills") from the correct position for control and awareness of the horse. Where I am positioned allows me to "read" my horse's body and actions easily (see p. 51 for more on this).

not get left behind and are moving as much as the horse. (See my explanation of position while longeing—it is the same for liberty, you just don't have a line—p. 36.)

I prefer to do liberty in an oval or square paddock instead of a round pen. Why? Because then you are not always going in a circle. Horses that are always round-penned have trouble going straight. Oval or square working areas allow the horse to sometimes go straight, and thus they learn better self-carriage.

I always use the centerline of our workspace as my guide—I want to walk as few steps as possible and control the movement of my horse without any sort of attachment. Moving him toward the corners improves the horse who tends to fall in.

LEARN TO USE TONE

The use of voice is very important when working with a horse on the ground. Horses do not understand words; they understand tones of words. A word or phrase that starts and ends in a deep tone indicates a command. "Whoa," "Walk," "Trot," "Canter" should never end with a higher-pitched or softer tone. When you say, "Whoa," and your voice gets higher and lighter at the end of the word, it "allows" the horse to do it when he wants to, as it seems like your command has a question mark on the end. A soft, quiet voice can reward a horse, or it can reaassure him, settle him, and give him confidence.

The length of the word matters, too. I will "make a word long" (draw it out) if a horse needs to make a quieter or smoother transition, or I will "make a word short and quick" when a horse is a little lazy or has lost his concentration and focus on me.

Your position on the ground, teaching your horse to lead without either of you pulling on each other, the horse staying parallel to you, and using your voice correctly are how you will gain complete obedience and manners in-hand.

You have to practice your voice commands with your horse and know how you have given a vocal cue and how your horse has responded. When you do not receive the response you would like, change your voice, change the word, or change your position to help the horse do it better.

Use the fenceline or rail to help the horse stay in balance and keep the same speed and rhythm in his gaits. When the horse falls in or out, losing his balance, he quickens his steps. (We do the same thing: If we trip, we quicken our steps to catch our balance.)

Working at liberty is a great way to see and encourage athleticism. You can use the horse's forward motion to have him practice flying lead changes

and do rollbacks to develop strength in his hindquarters. It is also a great way to learn how your horse likes to play! Tossing the head, bucking, and twisting are the ways he may need to get this healthy energy out before he can concentrate and be obedient (see more about the encouragement of "play" on p. 61).

★ **3. LONGEING:** Practice on the longe line is important as it allows us to develop control of the horse through responsiveness to verbal commands. Along with liberty work, this can be the beginning of using our voice and finding the right tones of voice that the horse understands to ask for walk, trot, and canter, as well as transitions within the gaits. This is not only

2.3 • While working at liberty, stay parallel to your horse and use both straight lines and curves. Position the whip as an extension of your arm to encourage forward movement.

exercise for the horse; more importantly, it is another way to control the horse's balance and encourage correct self-carriage.

There is an art to longeing the horse. Always walk at least one circle in-hand first, so if your horse is feeling good, he does not just take off in a hurry. You want the horse to gradually move away from you to make the circle larger as you feed out the longe line. Picture the handler as one point of a triangle: the longe line is one side, the horse the second side, and the longe whip is the third. To keep this position at the triangle's point while staying parallel to the horse (as with your in-hand work), when longeing to the left, you must cross your right leg in front of your left. When you are longeing to the right, you must cross your left leg in front of your right.

You should not walk toward the horse or back away. Control the size of the circle so you can connect the whip's position behind the horse. The whip should only swing softly toward the horse to encourage him to "move away forward." It should never be used in an up-and-down motion.

On the longe line you learn how to read your horse's straightness and balance on a circle (or lack of!). The horse must have his head flexed slightly inward, with his body following on a slight bend as it moves outward and away from you. If his head flexes too far to the inside, his body will swing outward rather than following the natural curve of the circle.

You will also find that if his head flexes to the outside of the circle, your longe line will actually get slack as the horse loses his balance inward.

It is common for horses to do either, especially "falling inward" on their stiff side. The handler must teach the horse to move outward by "rippling" the longe line toward the horse's head to encourage him to "move away" and do a larger circle.

Once the horse finds the right balance and bend at the walk and trot, ask him to travel on a straight line, still keeping your position parallel to the horse and moving with him by crossing your legs in front of each other.

Change the size of the circle, change gaits, and transition from a traditional longe circle to traveling on a straight line, and from a straight line back to a circle. This is how you can both recognize and advance your horse's self-carriage. You also learn to recognize when your horse is straight and balanced, how well he responds to your voice commands with eye

2.4 A & B • When positioned properly for longeing, you form a triangle shape: the horse as one side, the longe line and longe whip as two other sides, and the handler as its point (A). As you direct the horse at all three gaits, on a curve or on a straightaway, your legs should cross over as you adjust your body to remain parallel to the horse and in your point position of the triangle (B).

WHAT "TYPE" ARE YOU?

Liberty and longeing tell you a lot about the horse's *type*. I, of course, favor Appendix Quarter Horses, which are usually hunter-type, English-type horses. Identifying this helped give me a roadmap not only for their training foundation, but also for eventually building in two or three Western events for versatility (maybe Trail, Western Riding, Reining).

But in the case of these hunter-type horses, I always did the English work first *because of the horse's type*. A lot of people get a horse and say, "Well, I want to do this discipline or this class," and maybe it is Western so that becomes their immediate focus. However, they might have an English-type horse with a long stride, which may make it difficult in Western Pleasure (for example). I always get the horse confident and fit and performing best in *what fits his type or conformation first*, and only then add other disciplines, events, or challenges.

contact and body position on the ground, and how to coordinate your own arms, legs, and steps. These are all great tools for your riding.

I do longeing and liberty work with my horses at least one time per week. Sometimes, we will progress to a very short under-saddle session afterward, or the longeing or liberty by itself will be our training for the day. When you improve the horse's manners and obedience on the ground, you are setting the standard for all that you do together. "You are learning on the ground what you must feel and achieve under saddle," Ms. Steele would always tell me. "You are learning on the ground what you must 'feel' when on the horse."

★ **4. GROUND-DRIVING OR LONG-LINING:** This is necessary for all young horses to teach them to steer: right, left, stop, and back up. I believe it is a must before ever riding a horse! Then when you get on him and start to walk, steer, stop and back, you're not confusing him. (One of my goals is never to confuse a horse.) Older horses benefit from ground-driving because of its usefulness as a low-impact conditioning tool and low-stress

2.5 A & B • An important step in preparing the young horse for under-saddle work is ground-driving (long-lining). I like to do this in a side-pull. I teach the horse halt, back up, transitions, and turns, positioning myself on both sides of his body. This is also fundamental preparation for driving, which I like to do with all my horses.

A

training activity that adds variety to your program. Ground-driving also taught me how to help my horses develop straightness—being behind the horse, you can see his topline, his head position, and his footfalls.

Ground-driving is a great way to build a foundation of training, understanding, and trust with your horse. (I have an entire instructional video program on how to ground-drive—as well as other aspects of groundwork I'm mentioning here—as part of my "Longevity Training" series, available from LynnPalm.com.)

★ **5. Longeing and Bitting:** When my horses are fully confident and obedient on the longe line (p. 35), I add work with side-reins. I find them to be a great tool to develop your horse's straightness and balance without a rider's weight.

Before I talk about this, though, it is important to note that using side-reins is not for beginners or something that individuals who have no idea what they are doing should attempt, as you can do more damage than good and you can actually develop crookedness in your horse (which, as you know from earlier, you don't want!). Side-reins should only be used by those who have been taught to apply them correctly or who have professional help. They are an easy piece of equipment to buy and are generally accepted, so they can, unfortunately, be easily abused. People think of them as a shortcut to achieving collection, but it is not responsible to use them for that and that alone. They are for experienced handlers once the horse is already longeing very well. They are not meant to establish a horse's headset.

First, I always longe a horse left and right with a free head and neck before I add side-reins. (At shows, I often watch people put side-reins on a horse in his stall and bring him out to longe without any warm-up prior.) I use a surcingle that fits the horse well with at least two rings on each side and one in the middle of the back, and I always choose side-reins with a soft elastic section connected to the leather piece that attaches to the surcingle. This ensures a degree of "give."

Once my horse is warmed up, I add the reins, adjusted to a very light contact with his mouth. The inside rein is set one to two holes shorter than the outside rein. As I ask my horse to move out on the longeing circle at the walk, I assess the tension of the reins. They should be even, with the horse's head flexed just slightly inward and the outside rein showing the

2.6 A & B • This young horse is being longed correctly by my husband Cyril in trot (A) and canter (B). Note the length of the side-reins to allow for the horse to find his natural self-carriage.

same light contact to support a straight body alignment.

When starting a young or inexperienced horse in side-reins, the horse's head position should be so his nose is out beyond the vertical. After months of training, your horse will gain the conditioning to work with his head on the vertical, at which point you can adjust the side-reins another one or two holes snugger.

The horse should *never* go behind the vertical, with the side-reins too restricting. His neck should never look "tight," as this then tightens the back and impedes the horse's ability to engage the inside hind leg (which you want because it will promote balance while working "on the vertical").

I don't recommend using side-reins more than once a week unless you are working with an older horse that has been developed in a crooked way and needs a chance to figure out how to straighten himself without the weight of a rider. Whether you are longeing a young horse or re-starting an older one, the horse must be straight and forward in all gaits for side-reins to be of good benefit.

2.6 A–C • Our goal is to have our horses *on the vertical*, which means his forehead is at a 90-degree angle to the ground—that is, a vertical line (A). It is also acceptable, especially early in training, to be *in front of the vertical* (B), but we do not want them *behind the vertical* ever—whether doing groundwork or schooling under saddle (C). This is seen far too frequently in training and competition now and is *incorrect*.

They can be really helpful for the rider as they help her see the whole horse when he achieves straightness, self-carriage, and balanced movement. They allow the rider to see from the ground when the horse is relaxed and his movement gets fluid and consistent with a correct light contact on the reins. This is what you want to achieve under saddle.

★ **6. Trick Training:** Trick training is just fun! It is a means of interacting with your horse without involving stressful physical work. It is another great way to create and keep a good relationship with your

2.8 • My Royal Lark, learning how to bow.

horse. It teaches him to respond to commands and to expect a reward for correct behaviors. It is really important how you use treats for positive reinforcement. We teach tricks for fun, but they have a purpose, and the horse is still expected to be respectful and well-mannered, even when you are playing games. Horses want to please, and most enjoy the positive aspects of trick training.

Ms. Steele taught me how to train tricks with Nic Nack; I would go home and practice with my own horses and ponies. It was not only fun to do, but it was teaching me how to train horses, too. It doesn't matter what you are teaching a horse—a trick or to load or to half-pass. All of them require understanding what motivates the horse, and how and when to reward. Timing is really the universal lesson here. (I talk more about it later—see pp. 116 and 119.)

I taught Rugged Lark tricks; it was part of his all-around education. He could say "yes" and "no," throw a kiss, bow with one leg, "say his prayers" with two legs, lie down, and sit. The Lark Ascending learned to say "yes" and "no" and to kiss, which his owners loved!

Groundwork at Its Finest

Probably my best learning moment related to groundwork was when my husband Cyril and I went to Vienna during our honeymoon. We went to three training sessions and an evening performance at the Spanish Riding School. When I watched the Head Rider perform a solo long-lining demonstration, walking incredibly close to the horse's hind legs, no surcingle, just the two lines to the horse's mouth, I was amazed by his hands. They were incredible—there were no noticeable aids. The tempo in his and the horse's footfalls stayed the same. I watched them do half-passes at the trot and canter, canter pirouettes, one- and two-tempi lead changes,

THE TICKLE TRICK

Here's how Ms. Steele taught me to teach a horse to say "yes" and "no": It is natural for a horse to react with movement of the head and neck if a fly lands on him (he won't "flinch" his skin as he can do on his barrel and back). So I would tickle the side of the horse's neck with a hoof pick (as if I was a fly), and he would shake his head "no" naturally—and then I would reward him. I would tickle his chest with a hoof pick and he would take his head down toward the "fly," thus starting the up-and-down motion of "yes." When I got any gesture from the horse toward his chest, I would reward him.

So just teaching this simple trick taught me how to read the horse, use cues to mirror what might prompt a natural behavior, and perfect my timing in terms of stopping the stimulus (the tickle of the hoof pick) and offering a reward.

passage, and piaffe. Oh my gosh! I thought I did a lot with groundwork, but wow! I had tears coming down my face, it was so magical to watch.

Working in-hand builds perfect manners as well as the perfect movements I was privileged to see in Vienna. It provides the foundation for a happy horse who stays without being tied, and a horse who learns to trust you.

I will never forget one of the bridleless performances I did with Rugged Lark at the FEI World Cup competition when it was held in Tampa, Florida, in 1989—the first World Cup to be held in the United States. Raymond James Stadium, home of the Tampa Bay Buccaneers football team, housed the opening ceremonies, and Lark and I performed our musical freestyle right there on the football field. My opening song filled the air with energy. The stadium was packed with noisy, cheering people. I stopped Lark on the 50-yard line and dismounted, removed his bridle, then took the bridle to his owner, Carol Harris, where she stood on the sideline. I gave her the bridle, turned around, and Lark was still standing still, perfectly square, and did not move a step as I walked back to him. He stood like a pro.

HANDS LIKE A HEAD RIDER

The horse's mouth is the most sensitive part of his body besides his flank. If you want your horse to accept your hands, they must be steady and in the perfect position at all times. They should not, in any way, balance on the horse's mouth. When your hands are not in the perfect position, you will find that the horse will tell you so by resisting in some way.

What is the perfect hand position? The hands should always be positioned in front of any saddle and close to the horse's neck, not touching the neck but just above the crest. They should be held no wider than if you were to stretch your two thumbs toward each other, tips touching in the middle, and they should be held about halfway between vertical (thumbs up) and horizontal (knuckles up).

Hands held this way ensure the elbows are slightly bent and close to the rider's sides. If you run a line from where the rider's shoulder is right down her side to her heel, the elbow should be just in front of that line. When the elbow is behind this line, or out to the side, or has no bend, the hands are out of position.

Finally, when you look at a rider from the profile, there should also be an imaginary straight line from the rider's elbow through the hand and straight wrist, down the rein to the horse's mouth. When the hands are too high, too low, or too wide, you lose that straight line, and the horse says, "Ouch!" With that straight line, whenever you are communicating with your fingers on the reins, the horse is feeling that exact thing.

At a recent clinic at the World Equestrian Center in Ocala, Florida, British Olympian Carl Hester corrected every rider's hands. And when he changed the rider's hand position, he changed the horse. He was all about the horse's neck not being short or tight, and he was avid about the horse using his back and hind end correctly—and it all started with the hands.

We should all aspire to have hands like the Head Rider in Vienna or like Carl Hester's in the Olympics. You can improve your hands by improving your balance with lessons on the longe line, riding with and without the reins. Learning to balance from the seat allows the rider to coordinate where the arms, hands, and legs need to be, and what they need to be doing (or not doing).

Ms. Steele taught me how to ride without my reins with countless hours of lessons on the longe line. She would always tell me that if I could learn to ride really well without reins—walk, trot, canter, turning, and changing direction—that she'd teach me to ride bridleless, which was an exciting goal as a kid. But what Ms. Steele was really doing was teaching me to learn to balance through my seat and ride from my waist down. This taught me to communicate through my seat and legs more than my hands.

Practicing sets of shortening and lengthening the reins while riding without moving your hands or looking at your hands can be helpful. Do this first at the halt, then proceed to the walk, trot, and canter. Take your bridle home, hook the headstall on the back of a chair, and practice adjusting the reins in your hands while watching your favorite TV show!

A good rider and ground-driver (or long-liner) has active hands. These are not hands that you can see move, but they are hands that can adjust the reins smoothly when needed for changes of direction, upward or downward transitions, and adjustment of the outline of the horse.

RUGGED LARK
TWO TIME SUPERHORSE

BO-BETT FARM
7255 West Hwy. 329
Reddick, FL 32686
(904) 591-1020

When I got to him, I said, "You are the best and amazing!" Thousands of people were applauding and cheering and falling more in love with this horse by the minute. With all the noise and bright spotlights, I knew that any other horse would have exited the stadium!

Princess Anne, then president of the FEI, heard about our performance and asked that we do it again so she could see. We did so at the end of the event in the lovely arena that had held the jumping competition. Perhaps even more fun for both of us, Lark and I were asked to appear at cocktail parties throughout the long weekend!

2.9 A & B • I was so proud of Rugged Lark, standing absolutely still all by himself at the 50-yard line in the electric atmosphere of the World Cup in 1989!

2.10 • During the World Cup, Rugged Lark and I were invited to a lot of special events, so he had a neck garment that resembled the top of a tux and on his lower legs he had "sleeves" with sparkling cuff links. He was the hit of every party! (He preferred beer to champagne, although he had his share of both.)

MASTERING A LESSON IN A PARTICULAR PLACE AND ANTICIPATION

There's a secondary lesson when it comes to groundwork, and Lark standing still on the 50-yard line in a packed football stadium is a great example of how well it works. Bobbi Steele taught me the value of working a particular lesson with a horse in the same place until he learns it. When the horse masters the task in the first designated area, I move to other places to check and confirm what he has learned.

I especially like this technique for teaching horses tricks, but I use it to solidify all kinds of in-hand tasks like: ground tying, bowing, "saying prayers," lying down, sitting, saying "yes" and "no," Spanish walk and Spanish trot, turn-on-the-forehand, yielding over, turn-on-the-haunches, and backing up, as well as transitions, lateral work, and lengthenings, all using different dressage figures. I find it *always* works to teach the horse to perform a movement anywhere.

Practicing in one place is a great technique to make a horse comfortable with learning something new. With gradual repetition in a familiar spot, he gets to the point where he knows what he is doing, and then he does what many people would call "anticipation." Although you often hear riders and trainers refer to "anticipation" in a negative way, I think it is a positive thing. The horse is telling me he understands, so I know I need to be even *lighter* with what I'm doing, even more passive with my aids.

I love anticipation! A horse I was just working with recently did his walk and trot work, and all of a sudden, what do you know, he was ready to canter and anticipated that it was what I would ask for next. Well, that was okay with me—I let him canter, then brought him back to the trot, which was the gait I wanted at the time. It was okay because the horse knew what I was doing and was trying to give me what he *thought* I wanted.

"Reading" the Horse

Ms. Steele took me to many horse shows and events where I didn't ride; we would just sit and "read" the horses. She would have me practice noticing how horses were reacting to their riders—when they were listening, when they were accepting, when they were willing and relaxed or showing signs of resisting. Once she took me to a famous riding family's farm for a clinic—trainers who she felt were "whip-and-spur" riders who rushed horses and rode from the hand—and she pointed out how those horses were always "on the muscle," as she called it. They were always "tight," and she pointed out the other signs of resistance that indicated what the horses didn't like about how they were being asked to do things. "There is a reason for that," she would say after a movement of a tail or while noting a tight and tense mouth. She explained that the horse was trying to tell his rider something. It fascinated me. It still does today.

People don't need to be professionals to learn to look at a horse and recognize: *This horse is happy*, and *This horse is miserable*. Relaxed/calm and tight/tense are the first things you develop your eye to recognize. They are the simplest states of being in a horse that you can see. But I'll be honest: you can't learn to read a horse by looking through one book or having one lesson. It takes a lifetime of watching and developing your understanding and your eye.

> I can use that inclination on the part of the horse, which some might have called a mistake, in a positive way. I turn it into a positive by reorganizing what I am doing—going back, slowing down, starting over—and then always asking again lighter, or more with my seat and less with my legs, or whatever I can do to change the "ask" slightly, so the communication becomes more subtle. So then I'm not only teaching the horse a particular skill or movement, I am also teaching him lightness.
>
> Unfortunately, 99 percent of horse owners fault their horses for anticipating. But the horse is telling you he understands and is trying to please you. Turn it into a positive.

It takes time, but there is a simplicity in learning whether what you are doing with your horse is correct or not by letting the horse tell you. If you are doing well, your horse will be relaxed and fluid and doing things smoothly and in a way that looks like it is easy for him. And then you have the opposite—I've never seen a horse being jerked around and punished in Western Pleasure who looks like he is happy. Instead, he is tight in the neck, his body is tense, his ears are back, his mouth is busy, his tail wants to do something (but it can't). It isn't hard to recognize the signs of a miserable horse.

Groundwork, whether sitting and observing with Ms. Steele as I did, or working in-hand or longeing or playing at liberty, can teach you how your horse "talks" to you by watching his body. There are five places the horse talks to us: the ears and the tail (the most visible); the mouth; the eyes; and the general body stance and gestures. These are five reasons why groundwork comes first when working with horses. I learn about my horse and what he is saying on the ground. We don't have the same breadth of vision from the saddle—we just see the back of the horse's head and the top of his neck. We need to take the vision we develop on the ground and translate it into feel—into what we sense through bodily contact when we ride. You will then better understand what your horse is saying to you under saddle.

Whenever you are not making progress with your horse under saddle, go back to ground training and "read" your horse with your eye to find some possible reasons why you may not be making progress under saddle. If your horse is better without a rider (performs a task more willingly, for example), you know you need to find a way to improve your riding position or balance, or how you are using your aids (see chapter 3, p. 107 for more about this). If the problem is still evident on the ground, more time should be spent trying to discover the cause.

The horse "talks" to us with his body, so I think it is just fun to try to "read" him. Understanding his gestures and studying the parts of his body will give you "words" that he is saying. Even while you are riding, this is happening: You can see his ears and you can hear his mouth and tail. You must refine your senses to read them. For example:

★ **Ears:** *They tell me where the horse's eyes are looking.*

- When the ears move quickly forward and back, they are alarmed or worried, not confident, or they tell me the horse is full of unsafe energy.

- When the ears move slowly, they are confident and attentive to the surroundings or handler.

- When they are upright but he is somewhat relaxed, the opening of the ears are facing the back of the horse, and the overall horse becomes tense, he fears what is behind him and wants to flee. (If they are upright but he is relaxed in his overall body, he is accepting but could be unsure.)

- When a horse is what I call "frowning," his ears come back like he is mad and he holds them there, but without pinning them against his neck. This can mean that I need to lighten or slow down my aids.

- When the ears are forward, relaxed, and working back and forth, I have what I want from a horse in performance, as he is showing me he is confident, accepting, trusting, and willing in his work.

★ **Tail:** *The tail is the second most important key to "reading what the horse is saying" because you can see it easily from the ground and hear it when you are riding.*

- In performance, when you see the top of a tail is relaxed and the bottom of the tail swings side to side, the horse is calm, confident, and balanced.

- The speed at which the tail moves side to side tells when the horse is irritated or when what you are asking is difficult for him.

- When the tail swishes up and down, you have a temperamental horse with lots of unwilling tendencies. This could be the result of incorrect saddle or bridle fit, poor rider balance and use of aids, or physical issues in the horse.

★ **EYES:** *A large dark eye usually represents a confident and trainable horse.*

- When the upper lid of the eye raises and the horse looks "bug-eyed," he is alarmed and worried.

- When the lower lid of the eye wrinkles—be aware, the horse is mad and wants to resist.

- When a horse has "white around the eye," he may be confident, but more than likely he tends to be spooky, overreact to situations, or be undependable. I believe these horses do not see well, as is the case with a "pig-eyed" (small-eyed) horse.

★ **MOUTH:** *A horse's mouth will be relaxed when it is healthy (that means both the teeth and the tongue). When the horse is accepting of the bit, the rider's hands, and his overall surroundings, it will also be relaxed.*

- Like the ears and tail, when the action of the mouth is fast and hurried, or opening and closing, you have a nervous horse who has lots of anxiety or is upset.

- When the mouth is moving but doing it slowly, it can be from a bit not fitting properly, a too-severe bit, teeth problems, poor rider hands, or because the horse is not confident in his surroundings.

- A confident horse that holds the bit with a relaxed mouth is my goal with all my horses. As I said, the mouth is the most sensitive part of a horse, along with the flanks, so a horse will perform his best when the bit is not too severe for him and the rider has soft hands and good balance. A relaxed mouth that stays shut at all times is accepting and understands.

- When I have a horse with a busy mouth, I may ride him in a side-pull, which is a bitless bridle. If the horse's mouth quiets with this change, I can begin to rule out some of the possible causes of the behavior.

★ **OVERALL BODY LANGUAGE:** *This is when I tell horse owners you don't have to be a professional to tell if a horse is accepting or resisting. A horse that is relaxed in his body and neck with ears and tail that move slowly is accepting, trusting, and happy with his surroundings and the tasks he is being asked to perform.*

- If you see that your horse is tight in his body and neck, with ears, tail, and mouth moving in fast or tense patterns, he could be confused, frustrated, or resistant.

- A horse that is crooked in his body position will find it difficult to work in a particular gait or complete a specific figure, which will cause him to resist. Crookedness in his body alignment during movements that are hard, like an upward transition, will cause him to "talk" with his other body parts—for example, his ears will "frown" or his tail will swish—so watch for what he is trying to tell you.

Every one of these is important, and how movement is made matters, too. When a horse moves the ears, mouth, or tail in a fast or agitated way, it can mean the horse is not happy with his rider. When the physical reactions from the horse are slower, it may be just as important for you to change your actions on the ground or in the saddle to make your horse more willing.

Look at your horse's ears, tail, eyes, mouth, and overall body language. Consider what each is telling you. Go back to groundwork on a regular basis

> **WHEN YOUR HORSE IS NOT DOING WHAT YOU WANT, ON THE GROUND OR UNDER SADDLE, HE IS TRYING TO TELL YOU SOMETHING. IMPROVE YOURSELF TO IMPROVE YOUR HORSE!**

to allow yourself the chance to study all the parts of the horse while he is learning or revisiting a lesson with you.

Have a friend take a video of you riding so you can watch your horse's ears, tail, and mouth to see what you can change about yourself and your riding to improve your horse. On the ground or with a video you can see what is going well and what may be causing him confusion or anxiety.

There is an "art" to this reading of a horse. I actually love this part of horse ownership! It helps me know what I have to do to adjust my training with every horse, to allow each of them the time they need to learn, accept, and be willing. If I don't have that acceptance and willingness, I have to change myself to better understand the horse.

There is a major thing that differentiates how I approach this from others: this is practical. Reading a horse from the ground isn't about spiritual connection (although of course you are forging a relationship and bond with your horse while working with him in such a way). It is about developing the timing and the skills that you can then use with great success in the saddle. It is groundwork with a purpose related to what you do when on your horse, whatever that may be. Of course, you can do groundwork and never ride, if that is what you wish to do, but this is steadfast—it isn't about trends.

Learning to read the horse will work for your five-year-old niece in a lesson plan with a pony, and it works with the Fourth Level dressage rider with her hot Warmblood, and it works for the retired rider and her elderly rescue who just needs regular handling and light exercise.

No horse ever graduates from groundwork. And no true horseman ever does either.

My Favorite Exercises on the Ground

Leading for Manners and Obedience

There is nothing better for improving a horse's manners and obedience than work in-hand. Your goal in this ground exercise is to lead your horse from an arm's length away, and then gradually advance to farther away, up to as much as 15 to 20 feet. Here are some guidelines to help build toward success:

★ Look at your horse's head to read where he is looking and where his attention is. (Review my tips for reading your horse, starting on p. 51.)

★ Stay perfectly parallel to the horse. Most horses naturally walk in toward you when you lead them as they (hopefully) do not fear you. However, you must teach them to maintain their distance by gently tossing the end

2.11 A & B • Practicing the basics in hand is really important to having a horse that is respectful on the ground and responsive under saddle. I incorporate mini lessons in a horse's daily handling. In (A), I ask Indian Harvest to walk on the lead without pulling. I position myself with my shoulder at his throatlatch to help keep him straight as my right hand controls his head. My left hand extends my dressage whip straight back, which, when combined with my voice commands, can encourage the horse forward. In (B), Larks Sweet Judy and I work on backing up straight without pulling on the lead. I use my right hand on the horse's shoulder for guidance and encouragement of the lead or longe line toward their head so they respect the space between you and stay parallel to you.

★ The handler must be in the correct position for control. Your shoulder should be parallel to the horse's throatlatch or his head. If the horse is going too slowly, your position is too far forward. To encourage the horse forward, move so you are walking parallel to his shoulder. To stop the horse, move in front of his head (staying parallel to him), and lift the hand closest to the horse in front of his head so it "blocks" him, without pulling on the lead.

★ The horse must also move forward without you pulling on the lead rope. Your hand again moves forward in front of the horse's nose, but this time to encourage him when it is time to move ahead as you adjust your body so you are back by his shoulder. The use of an in-hand whip—just letting the horse see it from the corner of his eye is all you need—can also help encourage him to move forward. Note that the whip hand must extend straight back so the whip's length is parallel to the back of the horse's hip, rather than his barrel.

★ Practice leading in this way on both the horse's near (left) side and the horse's off (right) side.

Standing Square and Tying

For your horse to stand still and square on his own without being held or tied, you must learn how to stop your horse straight, or straighten the horse

2.12 • My Royal Lark stands square, straight, and balanced, without being held or tied. I teach this skill to all my horses. Not only is it necessary to allow for safe and efficient mounting, it is valuable when on the trail, working cattle, showing, and performing.

as you stop. You still use the hand up as described on p. 58, combined with your voice, to stop the horse without pulling on the lead. Once you stop the horse, you want the legs to be relatively "square" (front and hind legs even). When the horse is straight, he will balance himself square. The best way to see this is to stand in front of the horse and align his spine straight. If it is not, move backward and allow the horse to walk forward and straighten.

Once he halts with his spine straight, note whether the hind legs are in line with the front legs. If not, practice squaring the hind legs first. To square, keep the hind leg on the side closest to you stationary, and move the opposite hind leg to square via a forward step with a slightly downward tension on the lead. You will have to use the lead to "stop" the leg in midair to square. Reward the horse.

To move the front legs, use an upward tension on the lead and move the horse's head in the opposite way from the way you want the front leg to move. In other words, to move the left front leg, I position the horse's head to the right to take the weight off the left front and move it forward, back, or sideways from the lead.

You want to always square your horse using forward steps—you can use one step backward to move hind or front legs square, but not more than that.

Walk around the horse as he is standing square, rewarding him with your voice. Pet him everywhere until he becomes confident with the correct halt position and accepts it. You must be consistent with your handling here to perfect this.

Next, advance the horse to stand square on his own while grooming, bathing, clipping, and saddling. When he stands still, without being tied, he is accepting all that you are doing, and being very well-mannered.

Note: Be careful not to let him sniff the ground! If he does, his sense of smell and the instincts that relate to it will break his command to stand. Do not pull on the lead to bring his head back up. Instead, use your toe to tap him in the chin as you say, "NO!" in a deep voice. Then reward with a "Very good!" in a soft voice when his head comes up. Gradually, he will learn to stand longer on his own.

"Playtime" on the Longe

I like to allow my horses to "play" a bit on the longe line, which I find really helps when I go to shows and I need a way to get a horse mentally and physically prepared to behave in the new environment as he does when we're at home. The point is to encourage the play in a healthy way—it is "controlled play." As the handler, you are still balanced and taking the lead. The horse is not out of control because you are providing a grounding reference for him. Learn to recognize "how" your horse plays. Some horses play by shaking their heads. Some horses play by bucking. Some horses play by going fast.

Play should remain an activity that occurs within the confines of safe behavior (you should not be pulled across the arena, for example!). Controlled play on the longe should only be allowed after the horse is solid in the voice commands. I actually start this process at liberty (see p. 32) before beginning to incorporate it on the longe line.

Prepare yourself for controlled playtime by holding the longe line with two hands. Control the horse's head by keeping him slightly looking

> YOU CAN USE THE SAME GROUNDWORK AND UNDER-SADDLE TRAINING WITH ALL HORSES; HOWEVER, YOU HAVE TO TAILOR IT TO EACH HORSE AS AN INDIVIDUAL. HORSES ARE HORSES, BUT THERE ARE NO TWO THE SAME!

inward; if his head gets to the outside, the horse can use his body weight against you and get away.

Keep your circle smaller than usual. This gives the horse less opportunity to get away and also makes him work harder so he'll calm down more quickly. I generally work at the walk and trot first—the canter is where he's the most apt to play. When we do canter, I let him go (as long as he remains in control) until he stops running and tossing his head and I start to see his legs slow down. Then I ask for the trot. I may ask him to go right back to the canter and encourage him to play again.

You learn from longeing that he'll play more going in one direction: usually on his stiffer side or the side on which he falls in more (see p. 16). After he's gone both ways, I'll test him again with transitions to see his level of energy. When he performs a transition immediately, especially slowing down, his "playtime" is over.

2.13 • This is a fun, staged shot with Kim and Tom Blanton playing the roles of judge and scribe for my book *Your Complete Guide to Western Dressage*. But look how straight and square my horse is! This is what you are preparing for when practicing on the ground.

— CHAPTER 3 —

PATIENCE NOW PAYS OFF LATER

*"The longer you take to train the horse,
the longer you will have with him."*

— Bobbi Steele —

One of the truths I learned from Bobbi Steele was that the longer you take to train a horse, the longer he will last. The more shortcuts you try, the longer it will actually take to train him. We all get in a hurry. It is a natural human impulse, and it is probably more common now in today's hectic world. When I was learning from Ms. Steele, I would go home and try all the lessons on my ponies and horses. When I asked them to do something sooner than they were capable, it would set them back and it would ultimately take me longer to train them. What I had to learn was that when you improve something even by small amounts, you are making progress. By taking your time, you may not be teaching the horse "more," but you are developing the horse's body, joints, and athleticism to eventually be able to perform more challenging tasks with ease and balance.

My first horse after Sugar and Honey, Cracker, was bought by my parents for $300, including the saddle and bridle. He was delivered in the bed of a pickup truck with two board panels on each side and above the closed tailgate. He was a tall chestnut, and very gentle and safe. However, he wouldn't pick up the right lead canter. He was truest to the left. Every time I tried to hurry up to get his right lead, it would set me back two training sessions or more. Ms. Steele would come to help me, and she explained that he would pick up the right lead if I could control his body position so his body was able to do it. She gave me suppling exercises and lateral work, which taught me what I needed to control in Cracker so he was better balanced and physically capable of giving the correct reaction or performance.

Like us all, early in my education I wanted everything "to be correct yesterday." However, every time I hurried to do something too soon, I failed with Cracker. Ms. Steele would tell me, "I see that you have not been patient enough to achieve the correct bend before the canter transition." She could tell this was the issue because of the actions of Cracker—for example, always falling in with his poor balance to the right. When I was patient and just worked on the exercises that would prepare me for the correct right lead (rather than getting the lead itself), I always got it! It took me months and months to improve Cracker's flexibility to the right, but once I did, he always picked up the right lead canter.

From then on, I understood that Ms. Steele was teaching me the quality of great horse trainers: Take your time. When I did, my horse would concentrate more, accept my aids, and get stronger. I had to understand that even though I might not be asking for the right lead in a training session, I was getting Cracker loose and flexible, thus straight in alignment in his body and balanced. When I did this, I always felt like I was riding a different horse: he was relaxed, fluid, smooth; the rhythm and tempo in his gaits were more defined; and I could manage more precise transitions and maneuver him more accurately in figures.

Knowing When to Slow Down

When I called Carol Harris, owner of Rugged Lark and other horses I had the honor of training, most of the time I was excited to tell her about her horses' progress. I learned from her, too, to be honest and tell of difficult times, as she understood the process and would always have valuable suggestions. When I told her that Lark was not doing something so well and I wasn't sure why, Carol always said that when faced with challenges, "Do nothing! Just spend time with him, graze him, turn him out, trail ride, and just let it go." A few days later, I would return to training with Lark, ask him the same questions and try the same tasks, and he would do them willingly.

There were other times that this was different: Lark retained lessons like no other horse I ever had. I had to be careful to go slowly so he would learn to relax, be confident, and most importantly, trust me. I had to say to Rugged Lark, "You are not supposed to do this so well yet..." and, like during the challenging times, I would stop my lesson and go trail ride or put him away for the day. Just "doing nothing," taking a break, and coming back and sticking to basics was always the best advice.

I had the privilege of training Rugged Lark as a two- and three-year-old, and in 1985 we had a great year showing. He was four years young and won his first AQHA World Championship Show Superhorse title. With a foundation of classical dressage training principles, Rugged Lark was becoming exceptional and was in training for eight different disciplines. He competed in Reining, Western Riding, Trail, Hunter under Saddle, Working Hunter, Hunter Hack, Western Pleasure, and Pleasure Driving. He was a true example of the AQHA motto: The World's Most Versatile Horse.

The second Superhorse title was not as easy as in 1985, as "it is always harder to stay on the top than it is reaching it." After winning the second title, I surprised Carol during the presentation of the Superhorse award. By that time, I had played a little with riding bridleless, which Ms. Steele had taught me back in Sarasota, but Carol did not know yet. I rode Lark into the arena without a bridle and trotted, cantered, did flying lead changes and a reining spin, and the crowd went crazy! Our spontaneous performance led to 10 fabulous years of bridleless exhibitions at all the major equine events in the United States, like the one at the FEI World Cup in Tampa, Florida, I told you about in chapter 2 (p. 46).

The Art of Doing Nothing

I can't emphasize enough the importance of knowing when to "do nothing" working with horses. "Do nothing," to me, means two things.

Turnout!

All my horses, all my life have had turnout time that allowed them to be themselves in their natural environment. Horses have to graze, move around in an open area, and have room to buck and play. And, most importantly, they need to have lots of room to roll. Keeping a horse in a stall most of his life will always bring out habits, many likely unwanted, that under "normal horse circumstances" he would not have. Ms. Steele impressed upon me, again and again, "How would you act if you were put in a room with four walls and a small window and had to stay in there for hours, days, weeks?" All of us would be thinking about how to get out of that room! The horse, too! Even when my horses have had lameness issues or sickness, they are turned out if at all possible. When a horse has surgery and has to be confined for some time for healing, I am a stickler for finding out how many times a day and for how long the horse can be hand-walked.

"Downtime"—in the form of turnout—is necessary for a young horse in training who seems fatigued or needs fewer training days and more "free-play" days. Turnout is also the answer for the horse who is making lots of mistakes or is inconsistent in his training (not retaining his lessons). Turnout is for the horse who has just traveled a lot, been competed over a number of weeks or months, or ridden on the trail for many miles. Turnout will help the horse who has lameness or sickness issues.

How long should a horse in one of these scenarios have off with nothing but turnout? The horse will tell you. It may be, in the case of a trainable horse, just a few days. In other situations, it may be a week, two weeks, a month, or even longer.

How do you know if it has been long enough?

3.1 • With Rugged Lark, giving a bridleless dressage exhibition at the Shriner's Ocala Livestock Pavilion. We performed together for many happy years.

3.2 • My Royal Lark playing and having fun and demonstrating his amazing athleticism! Turnout is a necessity for the horse's well-being.

When you start the horse back in work, how does he feel? Does he have good energy? Is he willing? Is he trying? When the answer is yes, the amount of downtime was good for that horse. If you start back in work and your horse seems frustrated, resistant, or unwilling, the horse needs more time as you figure out what you need to do differently.

Consult your trainer, veterinarian, and farrier—your "team" players. Have a friend record a video of you working with your horse and share it with your team to get their help finding possible answers to any problems, as well as guidance as to what you can do differently. This is how you can accomplish positive training.

REMEMBER IT NEVER ALWAYS GOES PERFECTLY! YOU HAVE TO HAVE CHALLENGES TO HAVE SUCCESS.

Spend Time Together That's Not "Work Time"

Turnout isn't the only way to rest the horse and "do nothing." Other "nothings" are ways you spend valuable time in your horse's company, free of the expectations of training and showing. I call this my list of "justs"—because we always want to "do" more, but sometimes, we should just do this:

★ Just hand-graze your horse and spend time with him. (And that doesn't mean making phone calls or scrolling through social media. Really be with him.)

★ Just give your horse a thorough grooming session and treats.

★ Just bathe your horse.

★ Just take your horse on a relaxed, walk-only trail ride.

★ Just do something different with your horse. Take him swimming!

★ Just take him for a ride in the trailer to somewhere new and hand-graze him when you get there. (No riding!)

★ Just take your horse on a walk in-hand around your property or on the trail.

★ Just ground-drive your horse, or teach him how to pull a cart.

★ Just let your horse be a horse!

The Solve-Everything Secret: Driving

I learned a lot of things from Ms. Steele, but one of the most important was how to drive a horse and how to teach a horse to drive. She drove her horses because in the Sarasota, Florida, horse community in the sixties, they had sulky races at the fairgrounds. (In fact, this happened at county fairgrounds throughout the United States.) These races wouldn't necessarily be with Standardbreds—whatever horse you had was fine to use.

Ms. Steele had a Hackney stallion who was a handful because he had been abused and undernourished when he was young, but she brought him around with patience and good care, and when he was healthy and strong, she started teaching him to drive. Well, I had an interest in learning how to drive, so the Hackney stallion and I got our start together. (He had very strong hormones, which also gave me a base of understanding for eventually handling stallions throughout my career...but that's another whole story!)

I just loved driving. It immediately started to teach me what a proper contact with the bit was—a correct one that the horse is accepting versus the one the horse is resisting or the one where he is losing confidence because I can't keep the contact consistent.

Looking back, that was the real learning experience, because it developed my hands. I also learned what straightness was truly all about because

3.3 • Sometimes you just need to do something different with your horse—like a relaxed trail ride with friends along for both of you.

3.4 • My team of Clydesdales taught me a whole lot about groundwork and driving. I truly loved giving sleigh rides—it was a wonderful way to enjoy the natural beauty of winter in the Upper Peninsula.

I was sitting behind the horse and could see whether he was straight or not right in front of me with my eyes. If he was tilting his head one way or the other, or if his poll was not in line with his withers, or his hips weren't in line with his head—all of it was teaching me valuable skills that I have used as a trainer all my life.

The more I kept the light contact, and the more I kept the horse balanced and straight, the more he would just float along the ground...and go fast! He loved it! And he was eager and really obedient.

The best part about driving is that it taught me another way to practice reading the horse. Yes, people ground-drive (long-line) to add variety to training and teach a horse to stop and steer and back up a few steps, and all that is good. But when you put a cart behind a horse and climb up into it, you'd better be smart enough to recognize the horse is trusting you, and you'd better be sure he understands your commands at all times. And that comes with the hands and with the voice. Reading the horse and recognizing immediately if he becomes insecure is absolutely necessary, because if the horse gets scared, he will probably try to flee from the cart, and you only have your hands to slow him down—nothing else. You certainly can't turn the horse like you would turn a runaway if you were riding him. In a cart, you can't ever get to that point. You have to recognize the quiver of an ear or a change in the mouth—you have to be so in tune to what the horse is saying that you can prevent the flight before it happens.

All this led me to teaching my ponies, Honey and Sugar, how to drive. And Sugar was so fast that I even got to take her to Tampa and race her against all the adults! Eventually I used what I learned from Ms. Steele to compete in Pleasure Driving with my all-around horses. All three of my Superhorses, all four times I won the title, competed in Pleasure Driving. Then I established a sleigh ride business when I was based in Michigan. I had a team of Clydesdales and let me tell you, they'll teach you something! I gave sleigh rides six days a week in five different locations—bonfire rides, fireside dinners, champagne rides—it was so much fun! Driving with your big, cozy coat and your hat and your Ugg® boots, and everyone has cocktails

3.5 • I teach all my horses to drive. This mare, Larks Swiss Miss, ended up being the perfect match for my friend and client Heidi Burkhalter, who showed her in Pleasure Driving in Europe with great success. (I tell you their story in chapter 6—p. 165.)

and fur lap robes while those nice big dry snowflakes float down from the sky—I loved it. Today, I still teach horses to drive because:

★ It adds variety to their training.

★ It is a really good break when you are working with a horse who has been showing a lot and has been on a strict training regimen.

★ I always have one to three days a week that are just about conditioning. Well, for conditioning, you can't do better than driving—for both mental and physical conditioning.

★ I like driving! It is a great feeling when you can control your horse with just your hands and your voice and he trusts you and responds willingly. Because believe me, if your horse doesn't want to listen, or if he starts to run away, there's nothing you can do.

★ I find that once horses are confident driving, they love it.

★ If I cannot ride, I can always drive. It is a great means of ensuring longevity for a horse who might not be able to be ridden or for a person who might no longer be able to ride.

Lessons in Longevity

To me, longevity is about the length of time a horse has quality of life and you have quality of life together. Horses don't need to be "fried" mentally by the age of three or broken down physically by the age of five. We have the experience and the veterinary, farrier, and bodywork care that should ensure many years of active partnership in whatever disciplines we choose.

My understanding of how important the "big picture" is in a horse's training (rather than just immediate goals) has built over a lifetime of experience with many different horses. Here are just a few of the lessons I've learned about variety in training, patience, and listening to each individual horse.

From Weanling to Ring of Fire

I got Mocha Dell, a Quarter Horse cross, as my second horse. I talked my mom into getting her when my dad was away on a business trip: There was a bay mare at the fairgrounds (all the local shows were at the fairgrounds when I was a kid) who was obviously pregnant, and I was just obsessed with the foal and when it would come. My mom and I would regularly drive by the fairgrounds just to see if she'd had that baby yet. Well, when the foal was about seven months old, we found out who owned her and arranged to buy her without asking Dad....

The owners loaded her up, alongside her mom, in the back of a pickup with wood slats on the sides (as they did in those days), and just dropped my new filly off and took "Mom" away—and that was the weaning. Mocha immediately jumped the makeshift fence I had set up and ran all over the neighborhood. All three of us (Mocha, Mom, and I) were freaking out! My brother and I and my mom put whatever we could find up all along the fence to make it higher, and I caught my frightened baby and put her back in her rough-looking pasture. (When he got home, my dad was a little shocked that we had bought a horse without talking to him about it first. But he just said the day I didn't feed my horses would be the day they'd all be gone. I knew I had to step up and take care of them.)

Mocha was my 4-H project horse and the best horse to have as a child growing up. We so respected each other. I took everything I was learning on the ground and in the dressage saddle from Ms. Steele and did it all with Mocha Dell. And because I did the all-around stuff with her, that led me to want to pursue multiple disciplines once I was interested in the AQHA. I was mostly around Quarter Horses in my part of Florida and their motto was "the world's most versatile breed," so that made me even more intrigued to try all things with Mocha Dell. She was my "guinea pig"—the one who started it all. Whenever I got in a hurry and expected her to do something right away or pushed her to do something new, well, I'd suffer a setback (just like with Cracker), and Ms. Steele would remind me that I had to take my time.

Mocha Dell taught me patience. (And she taught me that a horse had to come to me to get caught!) Her own patience and general athletic ability enabled me to eventually train her to be a beautiful English and Western pleasure horse, trail horse, Western horsemanship and equitation horse, endurance horse, jumping horse, driving horse, and trick riding horse. Little did I know that I was making an all-around horse…a true "Superhorse."

For years I'd told my parents that I wanted to be a horse trainer "when I grew up." They allowed me to use the money that had been put away for my college education to go to a private college prep school called Golden Hills Academy in Ocala, Florida, where they had a horse program. Mocha Dell and I had the best year together at school—we worked on improving our over-fences and my equitation skills. The riding instructor there, Mr. Olsen, was talented in many ways and also booked entertainment acts featuring horses in the summer months when school was off. He and I got along very well, and he let me ride his registered Quarter Horse stallion after school hours.

3.6 A & B • I was so excited for my summer at Frontier Town in Upstate New York, where I was hired to ride a stallion through a "ring of fire" (A). Because I had practiced all aspects of the performances with my own horse, Mocha Dell (B), she easily stepped into the starring role when the stallion grew bored and sour.

Mr. Olsen wished to have an act where his stallion jumped through a revolving hoop of fire. At that time (1970), no one was doing such an act, especially with a stallion. Long story short, Mr. Olsen and I perfected the ring of fire, and he got me and his horse a job in Upstate New York for the summer at a place called "Frontier Town." It was an Old West tourist attraction with fake shootouts on the Main Street, robberies on the train, and a "Wild West" show and rodeo, which was to feature our act. I would jump into the arena, canter around, and jump through the ring. Then, two men would light the ring on fire and make the hoop revolve, and I jumped the stallion through it at just the right time before stopping the horse in front of the crowd, where he bowed. It was a hit with audiences and hugely fun for me. I was thrilled to be following in my mentor Ms. Steele's footsteps as an entertainer.

Then, a few weeks into our two-and-a-half-month contract, the stallion began getting a little sour from all the performing. Mr. Olsen had allowed me to bring Mocha Dell, my two gray Persian cats, and a sweet tame alligator (you read that right!) I called "Allie" that I'd purchased at a Florida tourist attraction with us to New York. It occurred to all that Mocha Dell might be a backup horse for our act. My mare jumped very well, but I had never exposed her to fire. Our years of training together, however, and of my trying all the lessons Ms. Steele had taught me on Mocha Dell, meant that the mare completely trusted me. She was also absolutely responsive from the progressive groundwork and dressage training we had done. It did not take her long at all to jump through that ring of fire with confidence. We were able to finish our contract at Frontier Town, and Mocha Dell was the star.

Learning how to trick ride was also really exciting for me—I was a wild, crazy, horse-loving girl and had to try everything. But the best part was that taking the time to bring my horse along slowly had paid off. She became a willing accomplice in anything I wanted to try, and eventually, a perfect schoolmaster for others to learn on.

★ *LONGEVITY LESSON LEARNED: Take the time to build a relationship on the ground with progressive lessons, and the sky's the limit under saddle.*

A Spook That Taught

I met Carol Harris through her daughters as they both went to Golden Hills Academy. Her oldest, Allison, also showed the Quarter Horse circuit, so Carol usually had her eye on her daughter or on me, as we were the two who usually took home the "All-Around Trophy," which was given to the highest-scoring horse at AQHA events and was a big deal at the time.

One day, Carol approached me and said that she had a nice Appendix Quarter Horse gelding that she wanted me to train for her. I will never forget the feeling of that conversation: I was thrilled and felt on top of the world! The horse's name was Rugged Cash, and Carol mentioned very cautiously that he had some "sting" and could spook quickly and put me on the ground. Of course, I still wanted to take a chance and train him.

When I'd had Cash for about three weeks, I called Carol and told her all was going very well, and I thought the gelding would make a nice hunt seat horse to start his show career. Wouldn't you know, the very next week I was riding Cash, confident and well, but he startled suddenly, and just as Carol warned, I came off. The horse was so quick, I was surprised for sure.

Rugged Cash was a very sensitive horse. I knew I could get a sensitive horse to trust me with a balanced position and very light aids, especially my hands (see p. 137). I also gave him confidence by developing my leg position so it stayed in contact with his sides at all times, and I allowed the reins to touch each side of his neck, all the way to his crest.

My legs were the most important. On sensitive horses like Cash, they had to keep contact. I always told myself I had to keep "hugging" him with my legs, without gripping or squeezing. And then that light contact with the reins to his neck. Of course, there was contact to the bit also, but I made especially sure my reins touched each side of his neck, all the way up to his crest. My leg and rein contact are what can give any horse confidence when he needs it. When we address something that I can tell he feels insecure about, my aids get more active but not stronger.

They get more active to keep the horse on the track I want to follow. I don't care if I'm on the trail, in the field, or in the arena; I keep telling him, with my legs and reins and voice, that I'm there with him and I know what is out there and it is okay. Not only are my active aids to keep him on a specific path of travel, they are to keep his attention on me and help him be less concerned with what he is worried about. They can keep saying, "Let's stay straight, let's stay straight, let's stay straight…now let's do a transition." And then we can stop and I let the horse look at whatever is troubling him, and he is still working on my commands—not getting overwhelmed and just blowing through my aids.

These elements that helped Cash feel "safe" became my focus as I continued to work with him. Cash also taught me that I had to see, hear, and know my surroundings much earlier than him, as my awareness would also give him confidence. I had to look, listen, and recognize anything farther ahead on the side of the arena or along the trail that could possibly make him insecure. If I was aware, I could handle the potential problem in a positive, proactive manner, instead of a negative, reactive one. Me being positive always made those situations a little less of an issue, and then a little less the next time, and as time went on, Cash became more reliable.

Things can happen when you get on a horse—a tree branch can fall, a bird can fly out of a bush, a dog can come running out of a house. That reliability that we want to have in those situations has to be established by recognizing the horse is a prey animal and his inclination will always be to run away from what scares him. Sensitive horses like Cash, very smart horses, those are horses that are very reactive to things that bring out the prey instinct in them. But by looking ahead, with a positive and kind approach and attitude, it goes away. So many people, when a horse shies a little bit at something, just keep going! Well, then the next spook is a little more significant, and the next a little more, and then the next one the horse is running back home because he was actually out of control and not paying attention to your aids the whole time. Planning ahead and quietly dealing with things that cause the horse anxiety can be a monotonous part of training and riding, but if you do it patiently, the horse not only builds confidence in his surroundings, he builds trust in you.

With my adjustments and Carol's patience, Cash became a very successful show horse, which led to over 40 years with Carol as one of my clients. I also grew to love the "modern" Appendix Quarter Horse with the influence of the Thoroughbred in the bloodlines.

★ *Longevity Lesson Learned: The sensitive horse benefits from an aware and confident rider who can be both soft and assured in aids and position.*

The Tough Ones Are Survivors

When I was a brave 17-year-old rider, I wanted a registered horse, as there were more show opportunities that could build a trainer's profile (and I already knew I wanted to be one). I only had one more year to do it as a youth competitor, so I bought a registered Quarter Horse gelding, sight unseen, from a classified ad in *The American Quarter Horse Journal*. I remember the price was $1,600! Legendary AQHA trainer and coach Andrea ("Andy") Moorman took me to Texas to pick up the horse…but when we got there, I did not like him at all. The gelding had white around his eyes and was long-backed and small. I had no

BALANCED POSITION

As a rider, you need to have knowledge of the correct riding position, which is how you achieve balance. This position puts the rider in the middle of the horse's center of gravity, which is behind the withers in the middle of his back. It is a vertical position. From a profile view, you should be able to draw a downward line from your ear to the middle of your shoulder, middle of your hip, back of your heel, to the ground. From the front view, the middle of the rider's body and chin should line up with the crest of the horse's neck, with the rider's spine in line with the horse's spine. An incorrect riding position will stress the horse in some way because the horse has to adjust his legs and his movement to compensate for the rider's balance. Sooner or later the horse is going to start resenting his rider. Riding in proper position and balance is the only way that you can continue to get positive, willing, and more correct responses. I talk more about rider position in chapter 4, p. 126.

> ## POSITIVE INFLUENCERS
>
> ### – Dean Ames –
>
> I learned to be able to focus on a goal from Dean Ames, one of reining's pioneers. It was 1969–70, and reining was really just getting started. I had noticed Dean at the horse shows, and I liked what I saw. He treated his horses really nicely and with compassion, and when he rode, he always had a really relaxed expression, even though he was also very serious. That attracted me to him.
>
> At this time, I had just bought Claudious Bell, who had been started as a reiner. I asked Dean to come and see the mare, and he really liked her lightness and thought she had a lot of potential. She was a different style than the reining horses that were popular then. She had Thoroughbred in her background, so she was a little bigger, a little more refined, and she moved with a wonderful fluidity. Dean felt he could take my very special horse and do great things with her—and he did. He taught me that being focused could get you places: if you trained hard enough with a horse while also really working to understand that horse, you were going to succeed.

idea what to do, confronted with the realities of my purchase.

As we began our drive back to Florida with the poorly built horse in the trailer, Andy suggested we stop in Mississippi at a reining trainer's stable and see if he would be willing to trade the wall-eyed gelding for another, as I had no more money to spend. And that is how I found Claudious Bell ("CB"). She was a green reining horse. I had an interest in reining, as I did in most horse sports, but my goal when I got her was to mold her into more of an all-around horse.

I got home with about four months to get CB ready for the famous Florida Gold Coast Quarter Horse Circuit, but I found that I could not get her finished for the show ring in time. Rather than rushing the mare, Andy Moorman again came to the rescue. She contacted Dr. Eleanor Green, who loaned me one of her prize mares for the Circuit. I was so grateful for Dr. Green's trust—the excellent show record I had with her mare helped get me the show record and credentials I needed to get my start as a professional.

In the meantime, a man named Dean Ames who was a reining trainer came to see CB. He really liked her and felt she had great potential—he offered to train and show her. I had no money to pay him, but he took the mare anyway. Dean ended up competing CB a couple times and winning with her (see sidebar).

But then CB colicked. I knew I had to do all I could to save her and ended up taking her to

Ocala to Peterson Smith Equine Hospital, which was said to be one of the best new surgery centers in the area. The team there did an exploratory surgery on CB and removed a stone in her intestine the size of a softball. It was the first time any of the surgeons had removed such a stone from a horse.

CB survived the surgery; however, it had been done via her underline rather than through her flank, and it never healed properly. She had many hernias due to the incision site. I spent three more years and five additional surgeries in the best vet clinics in Florida to try and fix her underline so she could show again, but nothing worked. In the last surgery, I assisted my "country vet," Dr. Gene Thomas. Once she was under anesthesia, Dr. Thomas proceeded to take out all the mesh and other materials other surgeons had put in my mare to secure her belly. Then he sewed two pieces of garden hose across the repaired incision to help keep the weight off the stitches inside and outside of the incision. CB stayed in a small barn at Dr. Thomas's facility for months as he dealt with infection in her underline as her body continued rejecting the mesh and other materials from her previous surgeries that he had removed. Dr. Thomas said that what he hoped was that enough scar tissue would build up so that CB's barrel could support her own organs and she could even have a baby…although he felt her own reining career was over.

A year after this surgery, Dr. Thomas said we could breed CB. And she went on to have five foals, four of them by Rugged Lark. Her nickname at Carol Harris's Bo-Bett farm was "Stinky Belly," because there was always a little discharge from all her past surgeries, but she was a great breeding horse and mother.

It took me four years to pay off CB's vet bills, but I did. Every penny.

★ *Longevity Lesson Learned: When a horse is tough and has a strong will to live, that horse is a great one, in more ways than one. CB proved that to me and showed me it is always worth doing everything you can for a horse's well-being, because the value might not be in "right now," but somewhere down the road.*

Slow Down to Avoid Burnout

The Lark Ascending ("Larkie") was an Appendix Quarter Horse hunter type and a very good mover (see fig. I.2, p. 4). He also had a very good start by his breeder. I focused on under-saddle training first in the disciplines his conformation and movement were best suited for—Hunter Under Saddle, Hunter Hack, and Working Hunter (he loved to jump and was very talented in that department). I schooled with Shane George over fences, who, at the time, was the top hunter rider on the Quarter Horse scene and specialized in USEF/USHJA hunter events (see sidebar, p. 185).

The Lark Ascending was showing special talent over fences, but I also got my feet wet again in the USDF dressage arena with him, and even taught him to drive. I was feeling Superhorse potential in him but realized I needed to get him some experience in Trail and Western Riding to be truly competitive. He was a horse that loved his training and his showing—he always had his ears forward. I had to slow down his training and not overwhelm him with too many events so I did not spoil his positive attitude about showing. He was still a youngster—only five!—after all.

I chose to slow down training related to the Western events for a couple of reasons. One was that training over fences takes longer and carries a higher degree of difficulty. I spent more time "getting him seasoned" with the hunter disciplines, and of course, we did driving for fun. But while training to compete in Trail classes would not be physically challenging for my horse, I knew it could be mentally. I have found that if a young horse does not do well with the typical Trail class obstacles, he can get frustrated. This is especially true when schooling the required flying lead changes—eight in a row! Most five-year-olds are just mastering one or two, to change direction in the ring or on a hunter course.

At the World Show, 13 months after I bought him, The Lark Ascending qualified in six events and made the finals in four of them: Hunter Under Saddle, Pleasure Driving, Hunter Hack, and Working Hunter. In Trail and Western Riding, he made it to the top 20. Just like his dad, Rugged Lark, he was named Superhorse with no soreness of muscles or body, and all the time, those ears forward! I did not know it at the time, but he would be the last horse to win the title with both English and Western events required.

The Lark Ascending went on the next year and became Champion Small Hunter on the prestigious Wellington Circuit.

★ *Longevity Lesson Learned: Sometimes you need to slow down with an overachiever. Just because a horse is mastering skills easily doesn't necessarily mean you should push forward to the next and the next and the next. The Lark Ascending showed me that spending time confirming what he had learned and diversifying his training rather than being focused solely on progression could ultimately yield more success over a longer period of time.*

Finding the Horse's Purpose

Reason To Believe was one of my husband Cyril's Grand Prix jumping prospects. The gelding had developed a habit of stopping and spinning at jumps. We patiently took him back to the beginning of his training, starting over in the jumping ring with small obstacles, as we thought most of his problems were likely because his training had gone too fast and he had been overfaced.

Despite our best efforts to restart the gelding, he never became a confident jumper. Knowing he was unlikely to find success with another owner, who might also try to jump him, we decided instead to find another way to bring out what was best in him by donating him to a therapeutic riding center. Reason To Believe flourished as he gained his purpose in life, healing lots of kids and adults over many years.

★ *Longevity Lesson Learned: Not every horse is right for the job he may have been bred for. Considering each horse as an individual and giving him a chance to shine in an activity where he feels confident and happy is integral to longevity. Reason to Believe found his place when we recognized that jumping would never feel safe to him.*

Cross-Training for Longevity

Rugged Painted Lark ("Bruce") arrived at Palm Equestrian Academy at Fox Grove Farm as a very bold yearling colt in 1998. After he began his training in dressage principles and groundwork, he traveled with us to summer at our farm in Michigan each year while also beginning reining and roping training with Ted Chancey in Florida, Sandy Collier on the West Coast, and Bobby Lewis in Texas. In between, he was jumping and learning to drive, too. Because he was such a macho stallion, we did focus on working cow horse and roping. He really did well as he came along and never forgot the dressage basics that I started him with.

I actually had to step up the training process with Bruce, as we had to fill the performance shoes of his brother, My Royal Lark, who had been diagnosed with an illness that was affecting his ability to train and travel. Even though I moved more quickly than I might have with another young horse, I didn't take shortcuts. He was a horse with smarts and confidence, and so was able to quickly master lessons.

Bruce was soon doing canter pirouettes and tempi lead changes, and being ridden bridleless. His looks and performances got him featured on book and magazine covers, in television shows and commercials, and as an entertainer at numerous equine events, including the World Equestrian Games, the FEI World Cup, and expositions around the country—the most notable being the 2017 FEI World Cup, where he wowed audiences with the first ever Western Dressage Freestyle in an international arena. At the age of 22, Bruce got to show off his years of dressage training with a fabulous Freestyle at the 2019 Western Dressage Association of America World Show. In his last appearance, at age 23, he could still delight audiences, appearing at Equitana USA at the Kentucky Horse Park.

★ *LONGEVITY LESSON LEARNED: Once I corrected Bruce as we were completing a Trail obstacle, and he never did that obstacle very well after that, as all he remembered was the correction, which made him nervous. His reaction taught me to never correct a horse while in the middle of completing a movement.*

3.7 • Ted Chancey and Rugged Painted Lark. As a young, strong stallion, "Bruce" showed a lot of ability as a stock horse in roping and reining events. I had him spend time in training with various professionals I trusted to build out the horse's natural abilities.

3.8 • What an honor it has been to have a Breyer® model horse created in Rugged Painted Lark's honor! We performed at BreyerFest, "a celebration of horses, featuring Breyer models and the real horses that inspired them" in Lexington, Kentucky, many times. Here we are in 2007 with some of his biggest fans.

3.9 • At the American Paint Horse Association (APHA) World Show, Rugged Painted Lark and I did a bridleless exhibition to music.

Reminders for Longevity Training

What these horses, and others, have proven to me is that training for longevity is always worth it in the long run. And it doesn't have to be hard. Just keep these principles in mind:

- ★ 1. **VARY YOUR TRAINING** each day or two. Cross-train with under-saddle training aimed toward the goals for the horse: groundwork, riding bridleless, trail obstacles, hill training for fitness, and swimming, if possible. And as I told you earlier in the book, I like to teach my horses to drive, too (see p. 74).

- ★ 2. **DON'T DRILL YOUR HORSE.** It is true that horses learn through repetition; however, if you drill (for example, ride 20 circles without stopping), you will eventually lose the willingness of your horse. Horses hate drilling! Keep your horse interested in his lesson by changing directions (*lateral suppleness*) and doing transitions (*longitudinal suppleness*). Minding this Golden Rule will also help you develop your horse's concentration for longer sessions over a period of time. Changing direction and doing transitions often teaches the rider to think: think "in front of the horse" (see p. 107), think about being confident, and think about riding with accuracy and precision.

- ★ 3. **TRAIN "OUTSIDE THE BOX."** An arena or a confined area is the place to teach the horse something for the first time. When he understands and can manage the skill, do it "outside the box" where there are new challenges, as the horse's instincts kick in and he becomes more aware of his environment and on high alert. I learned over time that it was harder to have a horse do the same task well outside an arena. I trained my first National and World Champion in the woods of northern Wisconsin for the three months leading up to the competition. My horse was *very* confident in the ring!

3.10 • Rugged Painted Lark and I trot uphill.. I am a proponent for training show horses outside the arena at least twice a week. This change keeps them from getting bored and encourages them to be forward-thinking.

★ **4. Listen to your horse.** If your horse challenges you, he is trying to tell you something. Use your common sense and try to understand what he could be saying. Figure out what you can try to do differently to get a better result. I always start with a check-in with correct rider position (see chapter 4, p. 126). I know my position weaknesses and try to stop them from happening. Position problems can be as simple as looking down at your horse—when you do this, you will be late to direct your horse with your aids, and this will frustrate him.

★ **5. Turn your horse out** every day and give him at least one day off per week.

Training for Longevity

What can we do specifically to build our horses toward a long and healthy riding life? I recommend combining figures in your ring work, including figure-eights, serpentines, half-voltes, and voltes. ("Volte" is a French word for "circle," and they are usually only 8 to 10 meters in diameter.) All these figures with curving lines can be used with short straight lines to change direction across the width of arena, length of arena, or across the diagonal of the ring, adding variety and interest to workouts.

Lateral work is also important. Turn-on-the-forehand; turn-on-the-haunches; yielding on a diagonal track, straight line track, and on a circle; shoulder-fore; shoulder-in; renvers; travers; and half-pass are all maneuvers that help you establish correct collection. And, when you combine them in certain ways, you can improve weaknesses in the horse. (I explain in detail how to do all these exercises in my book *The Rider's Guide to Real Collection*.)

Here is an example of a training session that I might do to help promote longevity in the horse:

- Circles at 20 meters, 15 meters, and 10 meters. Spiraling a circle larger and then smaller. Circling with counter-bending, and then changing directions with the counter-bend of the horse.

- Serpentines of different sizes, starting with larger half-circles and longer straight lines and gradually developing the athleticism needed for the smaller ones.

- Half-voltes and inverted half-voltes (in reverse).

- Riding a shallow loop at the trot, keeping the horse in the same bend through the whole loop figure. For example, if you are tracking left, starting at "A," you bend your horse's body to the left through the corner and

3.11 • My Royal Lark in a half-pass. This is the most advanced Western dressage lateral movement (seen in Levels 3, 4, and 5).

across to "X" on a left curving loop. Then keep the bend left as you follow a curving track in the opposite direction, away from "X" to the right and into the far corner on the same side of the arena. This is a great way to supple the horse and is preparation for the more advanced movement at the canter—the counter-canter using the same loop figure.

- Changing directions through the diagonal at different sizes—the longest change of direction on a diagonal track is going from one corner of the arena to the opposite corner. You can shorten the diagonal track by instead going from the middle of one long side to the opposite corner, or going from the centerline to a corner or the middle of the long side. The shorter the distance of the diagonal track, the quicker your horse has to respond to your aids.

The Anatomy of a Training Session

How you structure workouts with your horse has a huge impact on his physical and mental development over time. As I've mentioned, one of my goals is to develop lateral suppleness: bending him like a banana *compresses* muscles on the inside of the bend and *stretches* them on the outside. I always begin a training session with big, long lines—both curving and straight—to help the horse get supple and loosen up. I gradually make the straight lines between my next curves and circles shorter. As the horse "becomes more athletic" in his workout, I can add smaller turns and still shorter straight lines.

The warm-up should include some time at a forward, active walk and trot, and when you achieve relaxation and more supple responses, you can move to the canter work.

Transitions work the longitudinal muscles of the horse's topline and improve the flexibility and strength of the hind leg joints. It is harder for the horse to develop the "uphill balance" we desire if his transitions are "downhill," so I am a believer in *lots* of transitions in a training session to strengthen the neck, back, and hindquarters, and to develop the engagement of the hind legs under the horse's body so they carry more weight, thus allowing lightness of the forehand (that "uphill balance" I mentioned).

This simple "Golden Rule" of a training session (transitions—lots of them!) is also the best way to teach a rider to think, evaluate, and improve herself and her horse. Best of all, they help you keep your horse interested in the lesson. Horses (and humans) learn by repetition; however, as I've already mentioned, if you drill a horse in the same gait for any length of time, you will lose the horse's attention, "try," and interest and willingness to do more for you in the lesson.

In between periods applying my Golden Rule, I cool the horse down with work on maneuvers that are not physically difficult—all at the walk: turn-on-the-forehand, leg-yield, backing up, turn-on-the-haunches, shoulder-fore, shoulder-in, and haunches-in. Lateral movements like these are absolutely necessary to develop the agility the horse needs to develop collection.

My Favorite Exercises for Fixing Common Riding Problems with Longevity in Mind

Heading Off "One-Leadedness"

When you have a horse that is one-leaded (favors one direction or one lead at the canter over the other), he is most likely losing his balance (leaning) inward (falling in) on the side where he takes the wrong lead. The weight on his inside legs makes it impossible for him to take the correct one. You must keep the horse from doing this with your inside leg, flexing his head inward while maintaining a slight outside rein to help balance him. Suppling him through circle work (see the suggestions that follow) in the direction in which the horse does not take the correct lead is a great exercise. Most commonly, the "problem side" is the right lead. Circle work to the right will compress the muscles of the horse on his right side and stretch the muscles on his left side.

Circle with Cones

* Set up four sets of cones to help mark a 15- or 10-meter circle. Set them in pairs at the quarters of the circle to guide you and your horse on the correct round shape as well as give you visual markers for when to use your aids.

* Trot circles to the right and try to recognize where the horse "falls in" or "falls out" (his weight is on his inside or outside legs). If you can feel your horse leaning toward the inside of the cones, your horse is falling in and you will not get the correct lead. When you can make the circle round without falling in or out, you have taken the first step to getting the right lead.

* I use the last quarter of the circle marked by the cones to ask for the lead and the others that come before it to prepare: Prepare to ask for canter from the trot, as the forward motion will help keep your horse straight and balanced.

* You must create a bend with your horse in the first quarter, or before you even start the circle, or you will not be successful.

* Target your eye on the last quarter of the circle, where you will ask for the canter.

* In the second quarter of the circle, keep the bend or improve it.

* In the third quarter, position your aids to keep your horse from falling in with your inside leg active and the outside rein a reminder against his

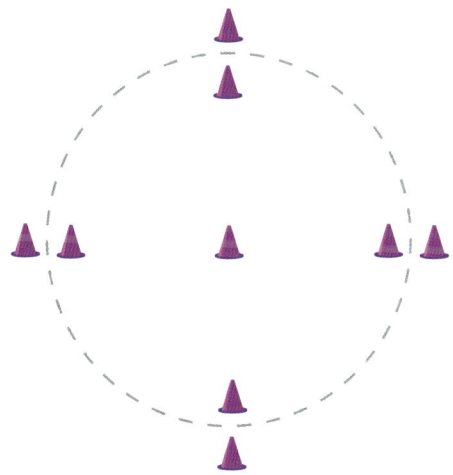

neck so he doesn't fall out with the outside shoulder and front leg and his head does not come too much to the inside. The outside leg aid should be farther back from the girth than the inside to encourage the horse's outside hind leg to start the canter. Keep the horse's head flexed slightly inward without turning on the circle with your inside rein.

★ When you ask for the lead, only canter five or six strides without your horse breaking before coming back to the trot.

★ If you get the wrong lead, move out of the circle and ride a few other figures elsewhere in the ring before coming back to it to try again. Do not get frustrated if you are not successful, as your horse will sense it and become frustrated, too. Remember: *The horse knows every word you are thinking!* Just repeat the exercise, as the circle work will continue to get your horse more supple, agile, and straight, all part of the correct balance he needs to pick up the correct lead.

3.12 • Use four pairs of cones to create a track for you to follow on a 20-meter circle and to mark the quarters to target when preparing and asking for your canter lead.

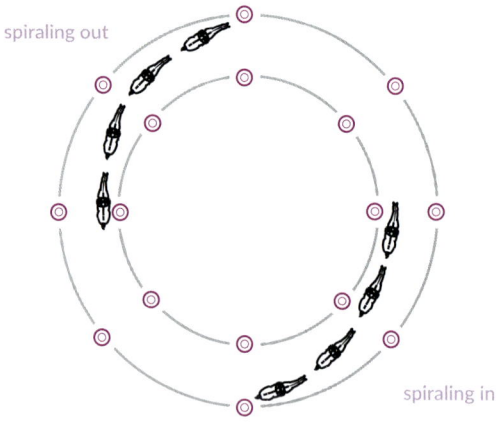

Spiral to a Straightaway

Here's another great way to help the horse who has difficulty picking up the correct lead. Again, we start at a trot on a circle.

★ Continue to make the horse more supple by gradually spiraling out to make the circle bigger. Then slowly spiral in. Then spiral out again.

★ Do not do more than five circles in a row, as circles are boring for a horse, and too many will "lose his try." I've said it before: horses hate drilling.

★ Next, extend the trot to a controlled speed. Do this both on the circle and on a straight side, too. Extending the trot helps the horse develop balance, and it improves your skill in controlling the horse's balance, as well as his straightness. You want to create an extension that ensures that when you are ready to canter, the horse will step right into the canter because you have the forward motion to help him do so.

★ I like to now add two parallel poles on the ground at the far end of one diagonal track, as you approach the short side. Track left and go across the diagonal of the ring at a lengthening trot. When approaching the change of direction at the short side, ride between the two poles on the ground to help keep the horse from falling in as you ask for the canter with your outside

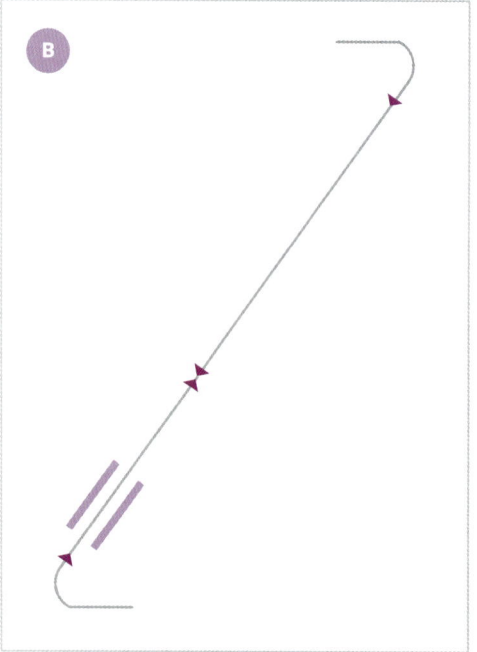

CHANGE DIRECTION OFTEN, CHANGE GAITS OFTEN, CHANGE SPEED WITHIN THE GAIT OFTEN.

leg positioned farther back than usual. Don't over-cue the horse. If you don't get the canter, or if the horse canters on the wrong lead, be patient and repeat the exercise. It can help to bring the poles closer together and increase the extension in your trot as you come across the diagonal.

★ **Note:** Do not "throw the reins away" when you go into the canter. Keep your contact to help the horse balance the push from behind (generated by your extended trot) and the lift in front needed to take the canter lead.

★ Once you are successful picking up the correct canter lead with the poles, widen them, and then eventually, eliminate them.

Livening Up the "Lazy" Horse

First, I don't consider horses to be "lazy," really. Instead, I say they are "not forward-thinking." I am very used to this characteristic, as the easy-tempered Quarter Horse is what I have spent most of my career training. Get

3.13 A & B • After spiraling in and out at a trot on a circle to increase your horse's suppleness (A), extend your trot across the diagonal to a pair of parallel ground poles at the far end of the diagonal (B). As you ride between them, ask the horse for the canter lead.

this horse out of the arena and ride outside! Trail riding, hacking, schooling in a field—all horses become more sensitive and less "lazy" in a more stimulating environment. The horse is a prey animal and will be more aware and sensitive in a more natural setting than in the arena where they have no fear. (I "train outside the box" a lot—as you learn in this book! If a horse is willing and well-controlled outside the arena, then *in* the arena, he will be as good or better.)

Do transitions often and change direction often. When your horse does something well, DON'T DRILL. For example, we all have a tendency to ride many circles trying to gain more control of speed or direction; however, as I just mentioned in the previous exercise, doing more than a few circles in one direction can become "drilling" to a horse. Horses hate it and will get less and less forward the more circles you do.

Consider this typical sample from one of my schooling sessions:

* Walk to trot, to lengthened trot, to slower trot, to walk.

* On a circle, then a half-circle, walk, to half-circle trot, half-circle lengthened trot, half-circle slower trot.

* Change direction through the middle and repeat transitions.

* Or make them different, for example: trot half-circle, lengthened trot half-circle, canter half-circle, lengthened trot half-circle, slower trot half-circle, walk, and praise the horse.

And maybe I am done for the day, or we go for a trail ride. The very best way to get your horse "in front of your leg" is to do frequent transitions. When the horse responds to your leg aids with more lightness and responds right away, reward him with your voice and move on to working toward the goal of that particular lesson.

B

Improving a Horse's Responsiveness to the Aids

You've heard me say it before: transitions, transitions, transitions! When a horse is not responsive to your leg aids, first, get out of the arena, as your horse will be more sensitive working outside.

* The transition exercise I use all the time is walk, trot, walk only three or four steps, trot again in a straight line. Straight lines help get your horse forward; curving lines naturally slow him.

* Continue the same short segments of transitions until the horse moves forward to your light leg aids.

* If the horse continues to not "think forward," use a firm tap of your crop or whip on his shoulder to "wake him up," then try the transition exercise again.

* Advance to walk, trot, walk, halt, back three to four steps to trot.

* Next, walk, trot, halt, trot, and (harder), walk, trot, halt, back five to six steps, trot.

* When your horse's response is even a little better, reward him immediately with a soft "good boy" voice so he knows it is right to "get in front of" the leg aids.

Reassuring Insecure, Worried, or Spooky Horses

The best and simplest exercise to address areas that might cause worry for a horse is to not let him avoid them. I talked about this when I told the story of Rugged Cash (p. 83)—I see most riders just keep on going when a horse shies away from something.

3.14 A & B • You have already heard and have seen in pictures that I believe in training horses "outside the box." You can do a lot for the horse's brain and body by working on skills outside the arena—on the trail, in a field, through the woods. Bruce and I are obviously enjoying ourselves here!

MUST-HAVE SKILL: TURN-ON-THE-FOREHAND

The first lateral movement to learn is the turn-on-the-forehand, where the hind legs move sideways (or laterally), the front legs take small steps, and the horse's body stays straight from poll to dock.

To begin, I teach the turn-on-the-forehand from the ground, using a fence as a guide for straightness.

- Stand your horse parallel to the fence, and move to his off side, between him and the fence—you should be standing on your horse's right side ready to move his hips to the left.

- Position yourself at the horse's shoulder and stretch your right arm straight to hold the horse's halter. Take his head slightly to the right, toward your body. This will cause his hips to go left. Position your left hand in a fist just behind his heartgirth, slightly below the middle of the barrel, where your leg aid will eventually be. Do not look at your horse's feet! Look at his topline, as straightness of his body position is a must for success of the maneuver.

- Ask the horse to move away from pressure on his barrel by moving his hips to the left. Your right hand at the halter will keep your horse straight and not allow any backward steps. Maintain his straightness as the right hind moves forward and in front of the left. Complete a 180-degree turn and walk the horse out of it.

★ My best exercise is to STOP in a parallel position to the object or area. And, if possible, you want to stop your horse before he stops on his own in fear, because then the horse is trusting you and being obedient to you. (When the horse stops first as he's confronted with something that worries him, he is in charge of the rider. When this happens, move the horse forward a few steps and *you* must stop the horse.)

★ Loosen the reins as much as you can while remaining safe. You know which way your horse will go (away from the "spooky" object) so you can be quick with your active aids (see p. 84) to stop him from fleeing. When you give him enough rein to let him swing his head to address the object, or turn him to face it, you are enabling him to see it with both eyes. This will help him feel more confident around it.

★ Once the horse takes a deep breath (wait for it!), shorten your reins and move forward, staying parallel to the spooky object. Don't try to get close to it yet.

★ Just as you pass the "spooky thing" (once his tail is facing the object—not too far), do a turn-on-the-forehand (see sidebar) moving the hindquarters away from the object or area, and again walk a parallel line, this time with the horse's opposite side facing it.

To accomplish a turn-on-the-forehand moving the hindquarters to the right under saddle:

- Apply your left leg on your horse's side approximately 2 inches behind his girth, cueing with the calf of your leg.

- Use an indirect right rein (the same as a neck rein) against the horse's neck to keep the front legs from going right.

- Put your right leg just behind the girth to keep the horse's body alignment straight.

- Use the left rein to flex the horse's head slightly to the left.

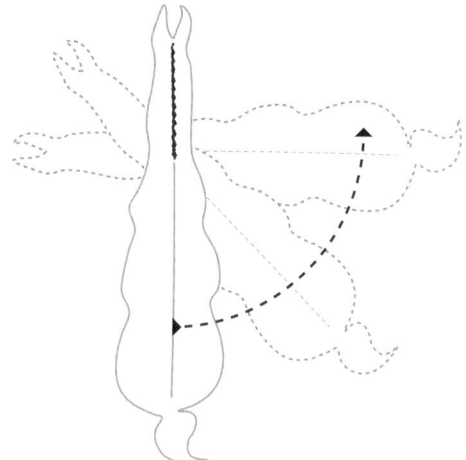

★ Stop again when just past, and do another turn-on-the-forehand, moving the horse's hindquarters the other direction and walking a parallel line again, but just a little closer to what the horse is afraid of.

★ Continue this pattern, using the turn-on-the-forehand until the horse, in each direction, does it slowly and without any backing steps.

★ Now stop again while parallel to the object and let the horse look at it on a loose rein. Then let him go to it and smell it, rewarding with a gentle voice and stroking his neck. His insecurity should be gone.

The same exercise can be done in-hand on the ground. Remember, when you have your horse at a stop, he must stand with a loose rein and not move his feet. If your horse moves one step—left or right, forward or back—when you have not asked for it, put him back the same amount of steps, slowly and with light aids. Do not get frustrated. Know that this slow and patient training will improve the horse's confidence, trust, and acceptance of your aids. In other words, when your horse "gets spooky," spend time with the source of the problem, don't avoid it.

3.15 • In the turn-on-the-forehand, the horse's hind legs move sideways around the front legs, which stay almost still.

POSITIVE INFLUENCERS

– Dr. Gene Thomas & Dr. Bill Sweeney –

I grew up with horses in an era when you did not show horses on a drug maintenance program or need a series of appointments involving machines and injections. I learned to manage with natural remedies, wrapping, icing, cold-hosing, hand-walking, and lots of turnout. These keys to well-being were instilled in me by two very important veterinarians I knew during my career: Dr. Gene Thomas and Dr. Bill Sweeney.

Dr. Thomas was the first vet to help me with my ponies and horses when I was a kid, and into my adult life. I told you about him on p. 87 in the story of Claudious Bell—he helped me get her breeding sound after her unsuccessful colic surgeries. She went on to have five foals, including the ever-so-special Phils Rugged Dancer (see p. 247). Dr. Thomas owned a local animal hospital and was a member of the Florida Veterinary Medical Association. He was also a breeder of champion Dachshunds and a life member of the Dachshund Club of America, as well as a Florida 4-H Club Hall of Fame inductee.

Dr. Bill Sweeney practiced in the Minneapolis/St. Paul area and was my go-to vet when I was based in the Upper Peninsula of Michigan. His equine calls extended from Duluth, Minnesota, all the way to Iowa, Wisconsin, Michigan, and Illinois. "Doc" was the veterinarian for the Minnesota State Horse Expo from 1990 until 2015. Doc eventually moved to Mount Horeb, Wisconsin, where he finished his career. He was an integral part of many of my World Champions and my Superhorses Rugged Lark and The Lark Ascending.

Both these special men would be considered "old timers" by today's standards. But they taught me and Cyril how to work together, often from a long distance away, by reading, feeling, and interpreting issues by phone—not by text, email, digital photo, or instant message. Cyril and I learned to be very independent and self-sufficient when it came to our horses' care. The knowledge gained from these two men was priceless!

— CHAPTER 4 —

THERE'S NO BETTER MIRROR OF OUR INSIDES OR OUTSIDES

*"The better you ride,
the better your horse goes."*

You've already heard me talk about AQHA Hall-of-Fame Inductee Carol Harris. There is good reason, as she was my longest client, from the mid-1970s when she sent me the first horse to train and show to the last one in 2018.

Carol had an understanding about the training of horses. She knew that time and patience were of the utmost importance for success. I've already told you about the times I would call her and tell her that Rugged Lark was not "getting" something I was trying to teach him, and she would tell me, "Do nothing. Turn him out, hand-graze him, or go on a long trail ride." It always worked—when we returned to training, Lark would do what was being requested.

It was Carol and Rugged Lark who also taught me that the better I rode, the better the horse would perform. They taught me this not only in the training arena, but in the performance and competition rings, too.

Improve the Rider, Improve the Horse

I talk more about being a better rider for the horse in the next chapter (p. 145), but there are three fundamentals to remember when training with the horse's good in mind:

★ The rider's correct position for balance in the saddle.

★ The rider's use of the natural aids: seat, legs, and hands, and in that order.

★ Controlling your horse's balance through straightness and connection, back to front, according to classical dressage training principles using the French techniques, emphasizing time, patience, understanding, and being an excellent rider. This is how I was taught and it is essential.

Earlier, when I talked about groundwork (p. 31), I first mentioned the importance of *timing*. Of course, "timing" when it comes to horses can mean many things, and they are all essential. We can talk about the timing of training a horse, and when to slow down, when to advance. In this case, I let the horses tell me when they are confident at a certain stage. They do so by responding with willingness, lightness, and balance. Thus, they demonstrate they have the fitness and understanding needed to do what I'm asking, and they accept the aids. The amount of time it takes to train is completely about the horse, and also influenced by the horse's age and soundness, and the discipline I am training for.

We can also talk about timing when it comes to the use of the aids. What do you use when and where, for how long? I use the aids in the sequence of: *seat, legs,* and *hands*. This applies for all upward and downward transitions, both changing gaits and changing speed within the gait. I use my legs and hands to control direction and the horse's straightness and balance. The connection of my hands and legs is constant but adjustable, allowing the horse to have the balance he needs to collect in different stages

4.1 • Carol Harris with Rugged Lark (right) and his World Champion daughter Jolena Lark (left). "If we practiced more bonding and less intimidation," she would say, "there would be very little need for the continual expensive vet treatments most horse owners are being forced to experience today. Also, there would be little need for the use of so many bits and gimmicks for training."

of development: long and low for the beginner, and gradually bringing the balance of the horse upward with more weight transferred to the hind legs and lightening the front. The set of the horse's head comes in time when the muscle behind the jaw loosens and stretches so the horse can break at the poll correctly and connect "on the bit."

We might also consider the timing of when you ask a horse to do something. I train my horses to be straight on both straight lines and curving lines, and that way whenever I ask them to do something, they are balanced and respond on command. I never try to do something when one of their legs is down or up—it is way too hard for them and doesn't set them up for success.

Timing in all forms comes with a balanced rider. You know what else does? Feel. A balanced seat allows the rider to feel more of what she is

doing and what the horse is doing under her. We learn this by watching and listening. Time and experience in the saddle also teach us to feel what our bodies are doing and what our horses are doing underneath us. When we are balanced, we can sense our correct or incorrect position. We are relaxed, comfortable, confident, and can control adjustments of the reins and legs and the hips to follow the motion of the horse's movement. (When we are not balanced, we feel stiff, rigid, tight, tense, worried, with little or no sense of control.)

When a horse is balanced, you feel him have fluidity, smoothness in transitions, effortlessness in performance, and willingness. Whether Amateur, Youth, or Professional, you are always looking to feel balance and manage it in yourself and your horse.

Tips for Improving Timing and Feel

★ There is only one way to become a better rider: practice, practice, practice!

★ I always tell riders when schooling their horses to *change direction often*. Doing this works on the lateral suppleness of the horse.

★ Ride a lot of transitions. They develop the horse's topline, and improve the strength and flexibility of his hind leg joints.

★ Keep many figures (arena tracks) in mind as options while you school. This teaches you to think, evaluate, and manage the horse *every stride* and to learn to feel and have correct timing of the aids in order to keep the horse balanced. Circles; serpentines; figure eights; half-voltes; inverted half-voltes; changing direction from the centerline, across the width of the arena, or on the diagonal of the ring; turn-on-the-forehand; yielding at the walk; turn-on-the-haunches—these are all "must-do" maneuvers to learn the use of aids according to your horse's responses. Practicing

4.2 A & B • On WTR Herestoyourhonor ("Allie") in a really nice, balanced working jog, which is required at Basic and Level 1 in Western dressage (A). The collected lope (B) is shown at Level 2 and higher. I can only help Allie find this kind of balance in performance if I am balanced in my position.

POSITIVE INFLUENCERS

– Jane Savoie –

What a thrill it was to get to know and train with dressage rider, author, and mental training coach Jane Savoie. I first met her on the horse expo circuit in the early 2000s. Jane was often hired to teach the dressage clinics, and whenever that was the case, I was always there to watch and learn. She had such an easy-to-understand and logical way of teaching the movements and fundamentals. She always made progress you could see with riders in her clinics.

One of my best memories of Jane was taking Rugged Painted Lark to her to have her help with his tempi changes. She found many holes in my training that I had to work on, and what she had me go back and practice—basics!—just helped my tempi changes.

Jane was not what is known as a "Dressage Queen." At clinics and expos, Western riders, amateur and professional, all loved her as what she would teach actually helped them make progress with their horses in their discipline, whatever it might be. She made everyone believe they could "do dressage" by telling her own story. She told me one time that in order for her to build her skills and attain her goals to compete on an international level, she'd had to work double as hard as anyone else because she didn't have the natural talent. She had the work ethic, the willingness to practice, the competitive drive, and she did fulfill her dream of qualifying for the US Dressage Team. She was honest about it because she knew that it was possible to set your mind to achieve a goal and go out there and make it happen, while there are others who may have it easier with far more natural talent who might never get out of the box.

I learned so much from Jane, but one of the best tips she gave me was to always ride with accuracy in my dressage tests. Accuracy alone could make me competitive, even with my "nontraditional dressage breed" Quarter Horses.

Jane was an amazing horsewoman—funny, witty, and she loved her dogs like her horses! Jane was always for the well-being of the horse. She was patient with them. That was the number one thing that attracted me to her. She also believed that great horses came from great riders. You need to teach the rider to be a better rider in order for any horse to perform his best.

any of these as "slow movements" will help you learn how to "feel."

★ Close your eyes. This helps you *feel* the riding and performance picture you would like to see. Being longed, with and without reins and without stirrups, is also a necessary exercise, and here you can more easily close your eyes.

★ If you run into trouble or face challenges with your horse, have someone video you riding him. Seeing the moving picture of your position (especially your hands and legs) can help you understand how you may be compensating in order to achieve balance. A video also helps you see whether your horse is balanced and straight, and how he reacts to your aids. You don't have to be a professional to learn how to tell if your horse overreacted or did not react at all to your commands.

4.3 • Hot N Royal in a collected trot appropriate for Level 2 Western dressage and higher. He can perform like this when I ride in balance, with feel.

4.4 A & B • It can be of great benefit to developing the rider's seat that she be longed by someone else, both while using the reins with light contact (A) and without reins altogether (B).

You have to have timing of the aids and feel so you can adjust to the horse's needs and understanding of the exercise. I learned this as a young rider when Bobbi Steele made me ride all those circles on Nic Nack (see p. 20).

Bridleless Incentives

One day I will never forget, Ms. Steele asked me, "Lynn, how would you like to learn to ride bridleless?" Of course, I said yes! She said that before we could take the bridle off, I had to be able to go around the arena at the walk, trot, and canter, both directions, not using my reins *at all*. Well, I practiced *a lot* and was successful, so Ms. Steele then taught me to ride with nothing but a rope around the horse's neck to help control his forehand. Bridleless riding was so much fun, and I was learning:

★ To ride with balance from my seat.

★ To ride from my seat and legs to control most of the horse in transitions.

★ To ride from my legs to control my horse's direction and body position, and to only *guide* with my reins.

★ To ride back to front.

★ To trust my horse.

I also learned that my horse performed better *without* the bridle than he did with the bridle—and this taught me to have great hands with my horse's mouth!

POSITIVE INFLUENCERS

– *Tim McQuay* –

In 1986, freestyle reining was introduced to the competitive reining world, and it instantly became hugely popular with both riders and spectators. Riders created their own patterns, incorporating a certain number of required movements, and choreographed them to music. I was fascinated.

Carol Harris let me have a horse to do a freestyle with, and I went to Tim McQuay to get some pointers and show a bit with him. At that time, Tim had been in the top 10 of most NRHA futurities since 1978. Well, I got to ride some of his horses when he was coaching me, and I'll never forget what he said to me: "Ride my reining horses like you ride your dressage horses." And you know what? It worked. I could ride those horses without any problem.

Tim McQuay was never one to miss a lead change because he rode his horses through the leg aids. He understood the need for the correct balance in the horse. The horse can't slide to a stop if he's not straight. He can't lope even circles if he doesn't have a proper bend in his body. Tim achieved his fine performances *not* riding from the hand, which you see in so many Western riders. He never did that. He was very light with his hands. And his advice made me very confident to ride with him because I could see our training foundations were so parallel. They came from the same dressage basics and fundamentals.

Good Equitation = Happy, Versatile Horses

Is how you ride important in the big picture of producing happy versatile horses? Absolutely! Rider balance is accomplished by having a correct position in the saddle. When I improve my balance on a horse in any gait, the horse *always* performs more willingly.

Lightness

And there's more: How a rider uses her aids influences the horse's attitude and good or poor response. Horses love lightness. When my horses respond to lightness of cues, they are telling me they understand what I am asking and what to do. When I work with riders that have no idea of what lightness is—they are gripping with their legs and seat, or strongly squeezing without knowing they are doing so—it is a lack of rider skill that needs to change for a better outcome. When I can convince these riders that lightness is an important goal and explain to them how to do it, I *always* find the horses respond in a positive manner.

Control of the Horse's Balance

The rider needs to know it is her responsibility and have the skill to control the horse's balance through an understanding of straightness and how to adjust the horse's body alignment through the leg and rein aids. When the horse is straight and aligned in his work, he is *always* more willing, smooth, relaxed, fluid, and responsive to the rider's aids.

Improving the rider's basic skills, her coordination from a correct position, her balance, and her understanding of what it is she should be doing (and may be doing) with her balance and aids can make huge gains in a horse's performance. When you can control the horse's balance and alignment on straight and curving lines, you will have a horse doing his best at the level his fitness and athleticism allow, and performing better than he ever has before.

My goal is not to train to "fix" a horse, nor to teach or coach a rider to "fix" a horse. I have found the most success when I work *to improve the rider to improve the horse.* An added plus when this is the goal is that it enables riders to gain the skills they need to train their own horses.

Five Common Rider Position Problems

There are plenty of things we can do wrong with our bodies when riding horses. Some affect the horse a little, and some a lot. Our goal is to only affect the horse in positive ways. Here are the five problems I see most often:

★ **1. Looking down**—I talked a little about this earlier in the book when describing ways to get the horse in front of your leg. Looking down means you are automatically riding "behind" the horse's mind and actions.

★ **2. Leaning forward with the upper body**—Often this happens because the horse's motion throws the rider up and forward.

★ **3. Hands in the incorrect position**—This usually appears as riding with too-long reins, or not knowing to (or how to) adjust the length of reins, shorter or longer, to keep the hands in the correct position and contact for the horse and the sport. Poor riders move their hands to connect with the horse's mouth, which results in the horse receiving inconsistent and unclear or late cues. Horses will challenge the rider with an incorrect hand position.

★ **4. Legs too far forward**—Some riders try to find their balance by pushing in the stirrups, which tends to swing the leg forward in front of its correct position in line with the rider's hip, shoulder, and ear. Rider balance should come from weight in the seat.

4.5 • I am proud to work with so many amateurs with a clear passion for horses and riding! Here I congratulate Heidi Burkhalter and Rugged Ranger for the amazing connection they established in a lesson.

Heidi Burkhalter
Rugged Ranger

★ **5. Being stiff and looking like a statue**—A stiff body cannot allow its various parts to work independently. For example: if you are relaxed with a correct rider position, you can coordinate your left leg to do something; your right hand, your right leg, your left hand, your upper body to stay back; your eyes and mind to think in front of the horse; your heels to stay down as you cue your horse—and more. When you are stiff, the many parts of your body needed in riding only work together, not on their own, and so cannot give clear and consistent cues or maintain the body's overall balance.

My Favorite Exercises for Improving the Rider to Improve the Horse

Position and Effectiveness

There are numerous ways you can work to improve your position and effectiveness. Riding at least four times a week should be your goal in order to make a positive change. For position, there is nothing I like more than working with a rider on the longe line. The goal should be for the rider to keep the circle round with her leg aids and learn to ride without relying on her reins. (I have 90 different exercises available on DVD and by digital download—see lynnpalm.com for additional reading and viewing recommendations.) In addition, riding without stirrups, both on the longe line and off it, can further improve the independent seat and the rider's balance.

As for becoming better at coordinating your aids, aka "more effective" in the saddle, I recommend setting up training courses that include a course of turns, circles, and straight lines, with cones and poles to mark lots of places to do transitions. Make up the course you will ride before you head to the barn. Write it out on paper, then set it up in the ring. Divide the course into three sections and work on one section per day, then put the course together on the fourth day. The course will challenge your balance and the coordination of your aids.

Here are three examples of training courses I have used for myself and my students. To use these courses correctly, the goal is to stay in the middle of the cones or poles:

Course 1

★ 1. Walk over the first pole. Halt between the parallel poles for 10 seconds. Walk over the second pole.

TRAINING COURSE FOR YOU TO TRY WITH YOUR HORSE!

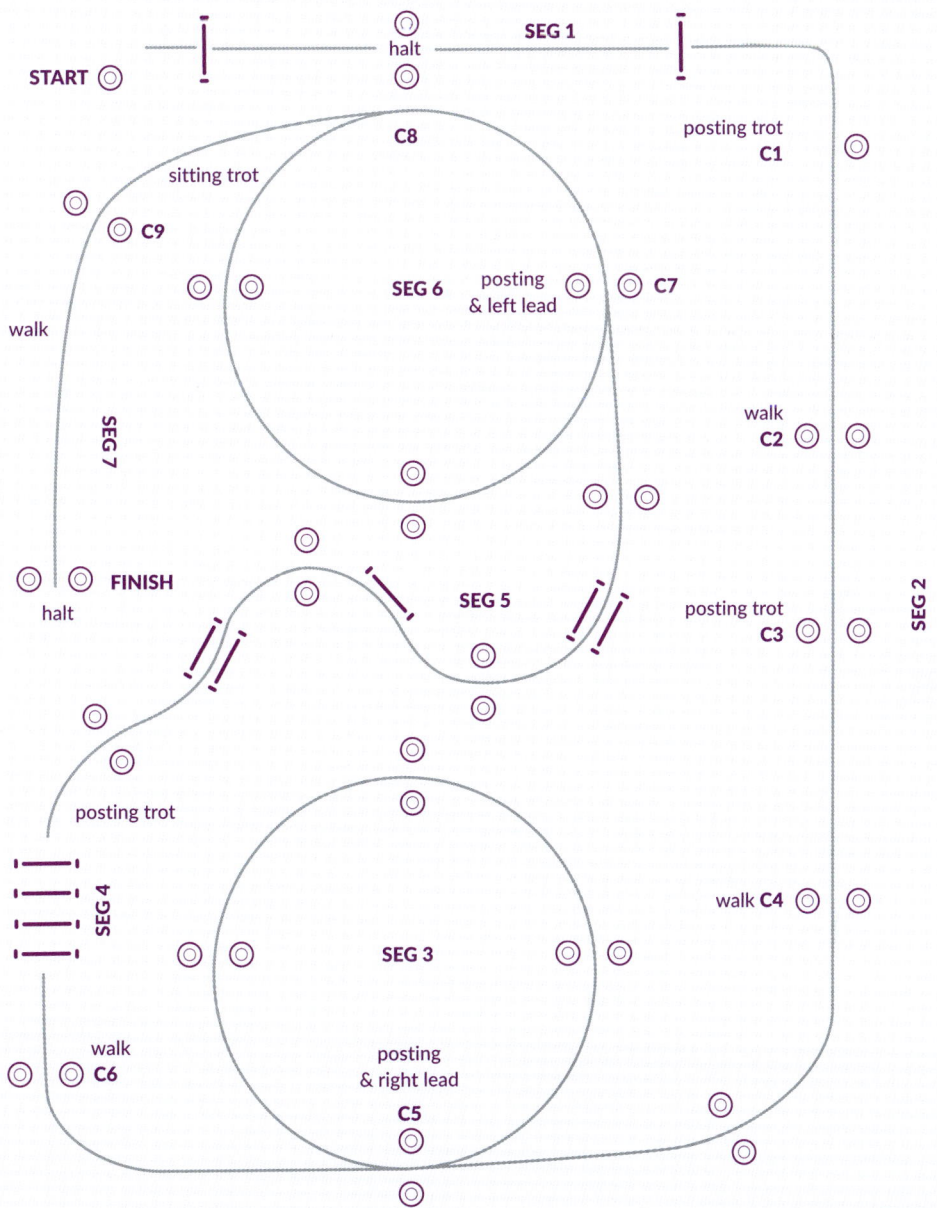

★ **2.** Transition from walk to posting trot at Cone 1, posting trot to walk at Cone 2, walk to posting trot at Cone 3, and posting trot to walk at Cone 4.

★ **3.** Full circle at posting trot starting at Cone 5, then a full circle right lead starting at Cone 5, then a downward transition to a posting trot at Cone 5.

★ **4.** Walk at Cone 6. Walk through ground poles. Pick up posting trot after walk poles.

★ **5.** Weave through cones and poles changing diagonals at posting trot.

★ **6.** Full circle left posting trot starting at Cone 7. Full left lead circle starting at Cone 7. Downward transition to a posting trot at Cone 7.

★ **7.** Sitting trot between Cone 8 and Cone 9. Walk to finish.

★ **8.** Halt three seconds. Praise your horse. End walking on a loose rein.

Course 2

★ **1.** Walk to Pole 1. Trot to Pole 2. Walk to Pole 3. Trot after Pole 3.

★ **2.** Walk at Cone 1. Walk ground poles. Pick up sitting trot at Cone 2.

★ **3.** Turn between cones and poles at sitting trot.

★ **4.** Trot-to-halt transition at Cone 3 (in a straight line). Pause a few seconds. Proceed with walk.

★ **5.** Posting trot at Cone 4. Cone 5 to Cone 4, lengthen posting trot on the circle. Cone 4 to Cone 5 slow down. Cone 5, left lead canter, full circle. Cone 5, posting trot.

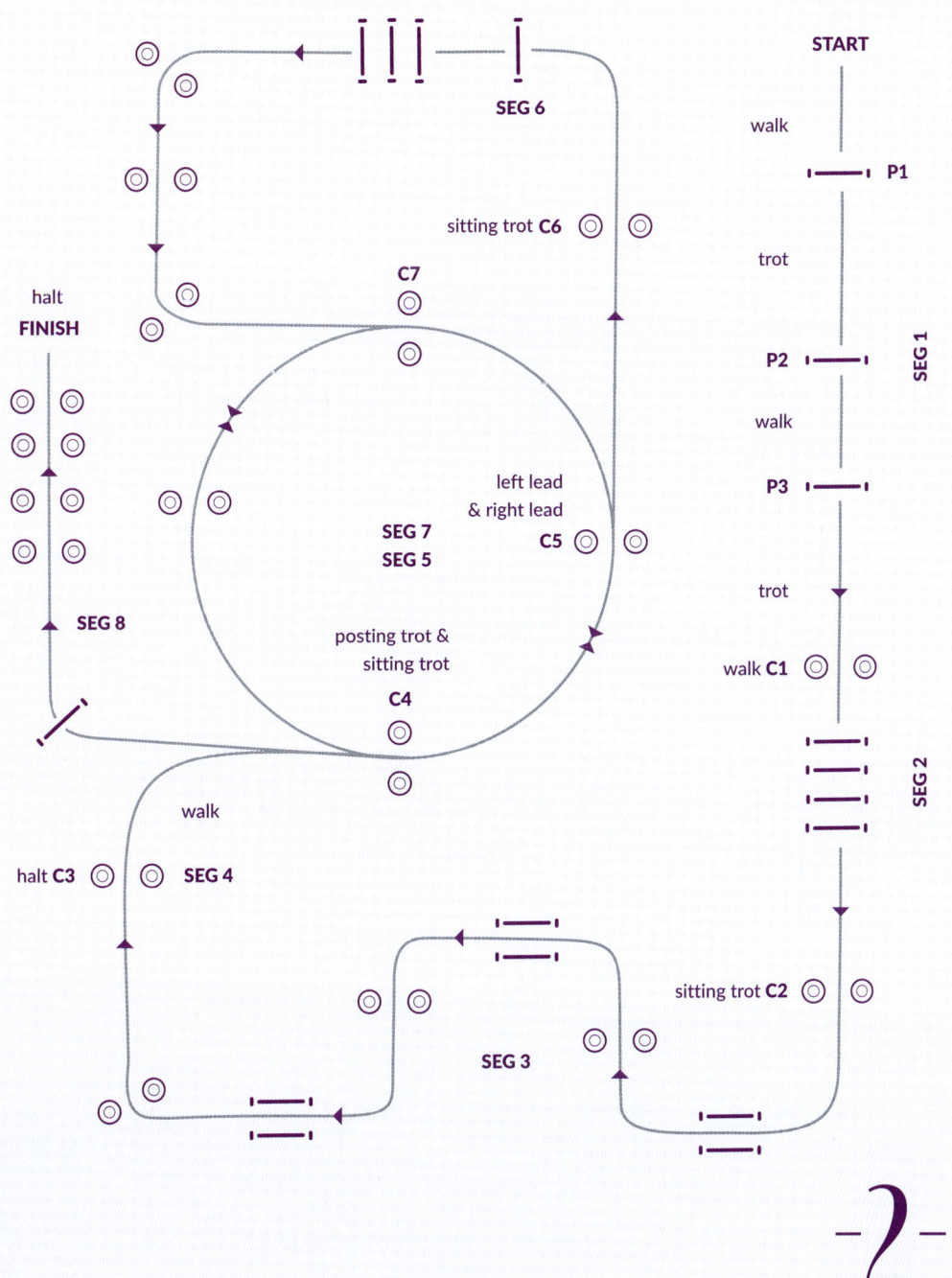

- **6.** Cone 6, sitting trot. Single pole to three ground poles at sitting trot. Left corner turn to left corner turn.

- **7.** Cone 5 to Cone 7, lengthen sitting trot on the circle, Cone 7 to Cone 5, slow down. Cone 5 right lead canter, full circle. Cone 4, sitting trot.

- **8.** Single pole at sitting trot, then through the chute of cones on a straight line at sitting trot.

- **9.** Halt three seconds. Praise your horse. End walking on a loose rein.

Course 3

- **1.** First series of poles at walk, second series of poles at posting trot, third series of poles at sitting trot, and over single pole at sitting trot.

- **2.** Cone 1, right lead canter. Canter over Pole 1 while completing a full circle. Transition to sitting trot at Cone 1.

- **3.** Take the single pole at the sitting trot, then halt at the pole parallel to your line of travel. Ask your horse for 180-degree turn-on-the-forehand—half to the right, then half to the left. Proceed to sitting trot.

- **4.** Sitting trot through the pole slalom.

- **5.** Cone 2, left lead canter on circle and over Pole 2, then maintain canter.

- **6.** Turn onto a straight line, canter over Pole 3, and transition to a posting trot before final cones.

- **7.** Halt three seconds. Praise your horse. End walking on a loose rein.

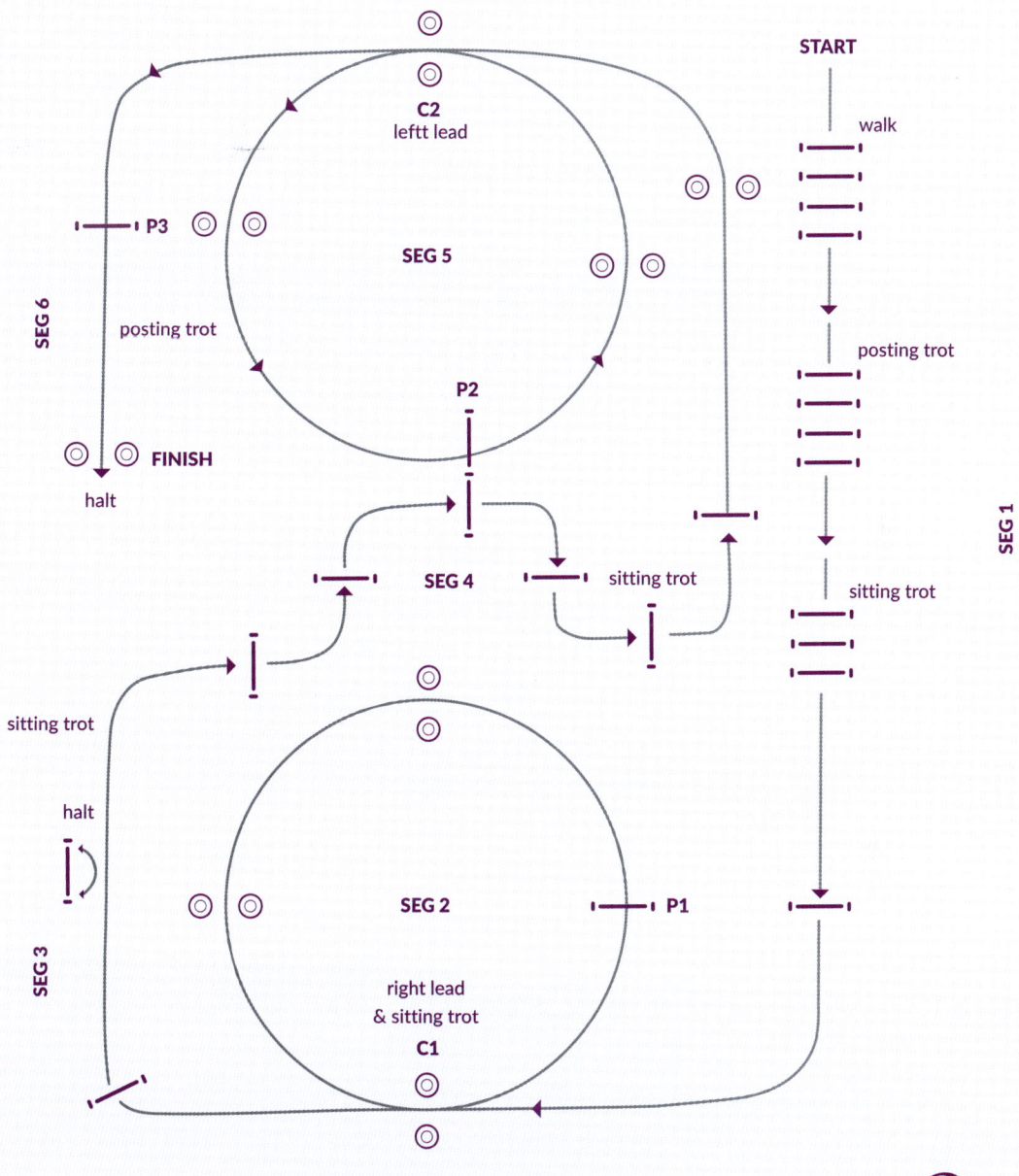

Fixing a Rider's Dominant Side

We all know ourselves as right-handed or left-handed. (Horses are too—we say a horse has an "easy" or "soft" side and a "hard" or "stiff" side—see p. 16.) As you advance your riding skills, you will learn that you have a tendency to lean to one side, and that on a curving line, you probably feel as though centrifugal force pulls your balance to the outside.

You will also find you have a "dominant" side when it comes to the coordination of the aids. Usually, your dominant side riding is the same as your dominant hand. For me, it is my right side, as I am right-handed. I have to be careful to not be too strong or quick with my right-side rein aid or leg aid, while I have to "tell" my left leg or hand to react.

Your horse will tell you which side is your stronger side by responding easily (or not!) to cues on your less-coordinated side and overreacting to cues on your strong or dominant side. You can also test yourself with this exercise:

★ At a halt, close your eyes and shorten and lengthen the reins without looking at your hands. Which hand moves more easily, and which one doesn't? You have to learn to "think ahead" of the weaker hand's use of the aids, and tell yourself to move it early. If your hand wants to pull or be overly strong, tell your hand to move forward toward your horse's ears or forward up his neck. This will soften and slow down a strong rein aid.

★ You *must not* change the correct position of your leg in an attempt to get a clear and consistent cue. Drop the stirrup on your strong side and close your eyes to learn to feel the leg in the correct position. Do not let the heel come up, which curls your leg upward and shortens it, resulting in a poor cue. Tell yourself before you use your leg aid to slow down and be as soft as you can. Move the leg slightly back on the horse's side and *don't squeeze*. When you get an improved response from your horse, you are succeeding.

4.7 • What About Lark loping over a ground pole in perfect balance on a curving line. The simple addition of ground poles or small logs not only adds interest to your training, it improves your balance, timing, and feel, and your horse's engagement and awareness of his feet.

- Another way to improve your dominant side is to have a friend take a video of you riding a figure eight. Have your friend positioned on one long side of the arena even with the middle where you will change rein. This is so you can see if you are pulling on a rein (usually the inside rein with the dominant hand). You can also see yourself on both sides and make sure your leg position is remaining correct, as well as your hands. Remember, correct position affects your use of aids and your ability to coordinate your legs, seat, and hands to ask the horse to do what you want. When the rider improves, the horse improves.

- You must not look down in this exercise. Keeping your eyes up will help your aids be more even both on the right and left.

- Work on thinking and reacting early and gradually with your aids. If the exercise does not go well, simply ask your horse to walk, consider what you need to do to improve, reorganize, and start over again.

Hands That Make the Horse "Heavy"

I mentioned that incorrect hand position is one of the most common faults I see in riders. There are many aspects of the horse's way of going that can be traced back to this fault. For example, the problem of a horse that is "heavy" in the hands. We must first assess the consistent responses of the horse.

* Does he pull "heavy" and then stay that way? This could be because of the rider using her hands to balance a little or a lot. A horse can get heavy to protect himself—defensive to the rider's hands. A horse that "roots" at the bit and pulls the rider out of the tack usually is a horse reacting because the rider is always holding steady on the reins or balancing on the reins. The horse is rooting to get relief from the pressure from the rider's hands. (See p. 46 where I describe the ideal position for the rider's hands.)

* It also could be because the horse has a poorly fitted bit—whether snaffle or curb—or the horse is not responsive or too responsive to the type of bit.

Once again the exercise that I like to use when faced with this problem (and you won't be surprised!) is transitions. They will help the horse push from the hind legs and engage under the body. This is what needs to be done to get his weight off his forehand. Upward transitions will naturally get the weight off the forehand.

You have to be careful on the downward transitions, however. Anticipate the horse to be heavy in your hands, especially if you tend to pull on the reins to slow down. Instead, bring your shoulders back, do not look down at your horse, keep your legs in contact with your horse's barrel, and use your hands with a soft upward tension on the reins to encourage the forehand to lift weight off the front legs as you slow.

Practice getting the sequence of the aids down—action with the seat, action with the legs, action with the hands—with walk, trot, walk transitions. I like to ride on a straight line and then on a curving line repeating

4.8 • Our goal as riders is to be balanced on our right and left sides. Because I am right-handed, I have to remind myself to be more "quiet" with right-side aids, and yet remember to engage my left side. Alotta Hope and I look straight and balanced in this picture.

WATCH THOSE HANDS

IT is far too common to see riders with harsh and overly strong rein aids, always pulling up and wide with the reins, thus sending the horse's head down to escape the hurt in his mouth and putting him on the forehand in his gaits. Other riders' whole focus is to get a "headset" from the horse. "Riding from the hands," or front to back (as opposed to correctly, which is from back to front with your leg aids feeding forward to light inviting hand aids), "blocks" the horse in front. The rider is basically saying, "Go forward into the wall!" This habit will develop a horse who is angry and resistant because he physically can't do what he is being asked, and it is seen all the time.

walk, trot, walk, stop, back, trot. Only do a few strides in each gait before transitioning, and take only three to six steps back.

As you advance the exercise and the horse gets more responsive and lighter to the aids, keep encouraging your hands to move forward toward the horse's ears in the downward transitions. Gradually shorten your reins so that any movement of your hands is invisible. You will then be using only your fingers to keep your horse from getting heavy in the hand.

BUILDING RIDER CONFIDENCE AND FACING FEAR

The possibility of a fall, and the fear that comes with that possibility, is something we all have to deal with, whether we have actually had a fall from our horse or not. It is on us to ride smart and safe. We *can't* fall—or, at least, we try not to.

I am just like all of you—sometimes the "smart" gets left home and I make mistakes that can be costly. "Riding smart" means riding with those who respect you and your horse if you are with a group. When alone, it means carrying a cell phone, or knowing someone else is close by.

Unfortunately, if you have had a bad fall, or if you have a really big fear of falling, your confidence has a hole in it. You can reduce the size of that hole, but it takes time and practice. In this situation, you also *must* be on a horse that is suited for you (I talk more about this on p. 182).

4.9 A & B • I like coaching students outside the ring. It opens up minds, grows confidence in both horse and rider, and gets the horse thinking forward. Here, we work on facing an obstacle my student feared: water.

STAY "IN FRONT OF" THE HORSE

When the rider is looking down at the middle of the horse's neck, the horse can "take charge" of the ride very easily! I say "the horse's mind is in front of the rider's mind" in this situation. This can lead to the horse taking one, two, or three steps without the rider asking him to, in a direction that is not the rider's choice. The next time it might be three, four, or five steps—and the time after that, more. When the horse is "in front" of the rider, the horse will challenge the rider more and more. This results in the rider losing control and confidence—and often blaming the horse.

Your horse is the first thing that can help build your confidence.

Ride in an enclosed arena, and before riding, longe or do liberty work with your horse at a high enough intensity that you see that his nostrils are flaring slightly and the veins have popped out on his neck. These two signs show that you have exercised your horse "from inside out." In other words, you have reduced any healthy playful energy that might increase the possibility of you losing control. Note that you *don't* want to tire him. If you tire him, you will be working toward a fitter horse that might need increased time and energy to prepare him for you to ride.

Your eye control is the key to that perfect balance you want on your horse. *Thinking in front of your horse* allows you to time your aids correctly, and *looking in front of your horse* is the start of refining your feel. These two things will keep you concentrating so well, you will improve your confidence because you will not be thinking about falling. Instead, you will be concentrating on your balanced position, how you are using your aids, and controlling your horse's direction and speed.

★ Set up four cones in your arena: one cone in the middle on each short side, and one cone in the middle of each long side.

★ Walk or trot along the rail, looking at each cone that you are riding toward. As you get close to each of the four cones, move your eyes to the next one.

"IF YOU ARE NOT POSITIVE ENERGY, YOU ARE NEGATIVE ENERGY."

– Mark Cuban –
Entrepreneur and Television Personality

★ After going once around the ring, change direction.

★ To advance this exercise, at each cone, do a circle of a comfortable size. When you have finished your first quarter of the circle, move your eyes to the cone on the rail and ride to it. *Do not look down at your horse or at the ground.*

★ After you have ridden a lap around the ring, with or without the four circles, ask yourself, *How many times did I look down at my horse or the ground?* The more you looked down, the less confident you are.

★ Continue to train yourself to "target your eye" and *think* and *look in front of* your horse. This will build confidence very successfully!

★ If at any time you feel like your horse is getting out of control, stop, reorganize, and start again on the path you were going.

— CHAPTER 5 —

THE COMPETITIVE EDGE SERVES YOU WELL, EVEN IF YOU NEVER SHOW

*"Success is made
of a thousand failures."*

My breakthrough to the national level as a trainer when I won my first AQHA World Championship was in 1976. My horse, Lecanto Raider, was an ex-racehorse who did not make it on the Quarter Horse track. Raider and I also won the first Quarter Horse Congress Hunter Under Saddle Futurity. That was a particularly interesting win, as my horse was sabotaged after the first round, but we overcame that to win the second round, and then went on to Oklahoma City for the win in Junior Hunter Under Saddle (see p. 199 where I share this story).

This wasn't the beginning of my competitive career, as I had always loved showing and performing, but it was meaningful in that I had moved beyond local circles and into the bigger pond. It also lifted my training at home to new levels as I began to strive to be successful against stiffer competition. I became a better, more attentive trainer and rider because of my competitive goals.

Here's something I don't hear many people talking about that I think is really important, especially when you are looking to your horse to give

his very best in whatever it is you love to do—trail ride, jump, Western dressage, working ranch, you name it. Even if you are just a recreational rider, you should *hold yourself to a competitive standard.*

"Why the heck should I do that?" you might ask. Well, training and riding with a competitive standard in mind gives you a mental edge, helps you attain balance in yourself and your horse, and provides a certain kind of simplicity to decision-making that can keep the waters of horse ownership from getting muddy. I think all this equals confidence, which the recreational rider needs just as much as the competitive one if she wants to truly enjoy her horse and all her partnership with him has to offer.

Let's Get Basic: Your Tack

One year I was presenting at Equine Affaire in West Springfield, Massachusetts, and in one of my sessions, I had a rider with a horse who was getting closer and closer to out of control. There are many challenges that demo riders face at Equine Affaire—the noise from the crowds and the loudspeakers, the acoustics in the large rings and indoor spaces, and the riders usually overtrying in front of the audience and clinicians—and they tend to create horses that are more tight and tense than usual. So I always start sessions by assisting the riders with different things that I know will help them get control of their horses.

This particular horse was gaping his mouth every time the rider touched the reins. I could also see him getting more and more tense and not relaxing or accepting his surroundings. I had the rider come over to me and I immediately could see the curb chain was way too tight. I carefully regulate curb chains on horses—they should be adjusted so they are at least loose enough for me to put my second and third fingers side by side and move them freely back and forth under and on either side of the horse's chin. Then, I always check the bit's shank and make sure if it is moved back to where the curb chain makes contact so it is *light* leverage, not *tight* leverage. In this instance, I adjusted the chain and the horse immediately started to relax and accept the rider's hands, and we ended up having a good session.

5.1 A & B •
Performing the Gypsy King at Equine Affaire in 2001. I've always loved performing, just as much as I enjoy competing. To do well at either, I need to respect the horse.

ENTERTAINING VS. COMPETING

The stories that Ms. Steele shared about her experiences as an entertainer and her times in the circus fascinated me. She would always say that she loved those who competed on horses, and she loved interacting with and meeting them, but as an entertainer, she didn't have to get wrapped up in some of the things that were more difficult about being a rider in competitive horse sport. Of course, the truth was, as an entertainer, she actually had to be as good or better at what she did than competitors. Because if her horses didn't perform happily, willingly, correctly, and with some uniqueness, she wouldn't get a job. It wasn't just about a ribbon.

She had a horse that was her canter horse in her performances. She did a stunt on the ground that no one else ever did. He'd be tacked up and she'd ask him to stand still and walk away a certain distance. She had a bamboo stick that was as wide as her arms and she would stoop down on her left knee, hold up the stick with both arms above her head, and she'd call, "Jump!" The horse would come, jump over her and the stick, stop, turn around and face her and wait for the next command.

Ms. Steele's perspective taught me respect for the animal in training, respect for the entertainer, and respect as a serious competitor because if a horse didn't perform *with me*, I understood we could never really be on top. Her success as an entertainer inspired me to try to be the best at certain things in competition, or to decide a specific horse could be a Superhorse winner—she gave me a drive to be unique, different, and to stand out. You get those kinds of inspirations indirectly.

Ms. Steele started her career with the circus as an entertainer, and I don't know that she ever competed herself. I, on the other hand, was involved with 4-H from the beginning, and competing was part of my "horse DNA." The 4-H had so much influence—the more you learned, the better you did—and why not compete because you got rewarded? So, competing had already been introduced to me before I ever even met Ms. Steele. Now I look back over my career as both a performer and a competitor, and I can say that I get just as much satisfaction out of competing as I do from performing, and vice versa. Because I was able to compete with the respect of, and respect for, the horse.

People just don't recognize the simple importance of how tack needs to fit the horse to be safe, functional, and comfortable for him. Appropriate and well-fitting tack is foundational to how the horse behaves and how he performs. The curb chain in the story I just shared was so tight, and the rider truly had no idea the chain was too tight, but the situation was escalating. It was the exact kind of scenario where a horse might balk and rear up, and that could have led to something both scary and unsafe.

Riding is a sport, and if you want to do a sport well, you've got to have the right equipment. Consider these basic rules:

★ Don't use tack if you don't understand how it works, the effect it can have on your horse, and how it should fit. Just because it is sold in a tack shop doesn't mean you should buy it, and just because you see one on another horse doesn't mean it should be on yours. There are plenty of bits, martingales, and training gadgets that people claim solve certain problems, but I can promise you, without professional guidance, most of them will only make a problem worse or create new ones.

★ Spend the time and money to have your saddle fitted to your horse. It is worth it. You will save both in the end. The way the saddle fits a horse affects the horse's attitude in whatever kind of performance the horse is participating. Think about it: If you have a pair of shoes that are too small or pinch in some way, but you go ahead and wear them, it isn't going to be too long before your feet start to hurt. Or, when you wear high heels out one night but you never usually wear them—you might be good for the first half hour, and then you're just wondering, *When can I take these gosh-darned shoes off?*

That is what happens with a horse and his saddle. What I see a lot with Western horses, especially, but sometimes English too, is that the tree of the saddle is too narrow in the horse's shoulder area and withers. (This is a common issue, but there are plenty of others—a skirt that is too long for

MINK OIL MAGIC

I personally have a slight obsession with mink oil. It is everywhere in my life. It is like how some people are with ChapStick®—you know, the people who have one in their jacket, one in their purse, one in their glove compartment. I use mink oil on all my tack and all my boots. It is a trick I learned from the great horseman and hunter-jumper rider Scott Hofstetter (he was ASPCA Maclay National Champion in 1986 and now is a well-known judge). Not only does mink oil really condition leather, it keeps it from drying out. It is also almost like a barrier, as it keeps moisture and water out, and prevents mildew. Because of my mink oil habit, I don't mind if my riding boots get mud on them—I know I can just rinse them off with the hose because mink oil gives them water resistance. Mink oil—I'm a believer.

the horse's back or English panels that are too narrow.) Think again about how uncomfortable you would be trying to run or dance in shoes that don't fit, and you'll understand that poor saddle fit can be why a horse is challenging you in some way.

★ Have a common-sense tack check that you use every time you tack up and before you get on. I always check my tack before I get on. Make sure the bridle is *even* on the horse's head, and the bit, curb strap, and throatlatch are properly fitted. Review your saddle's position and tighten your girth. This has to do with adjusting fit appropriately, and it also has to do with the condition of leather and strings and webbing. Tack ages, and if not well cared for, it can deteriorate and become unsafe.

★ With the above in mind, take care of your equipment. Regularly clean your tack. This makes it more comfortable for you and your horse; it preserves its quality, ensuring your safety; and it contributes to the image you project for others, and for yourself. This is part of the competitive edge that can help you even if you don't show. Would you ride into a ring in front of judges and spectators with dried green

5.2 • It is so important that what you wear while riding fits you well and is something you are comfortable in. This goes for competing, as I am in this Western dressage class with Sucha Fine Knockout or schooling at home.

slime on your bit and a sweat-stained saddle pad? You shouldn't do it at home, either. It shows respect for yourself, for your riding, and for your horse.

Professional Turnout

You don't have to be a professional to look professional. Clean and cared-for tack is a great starting point. It's also so important to have clothes that fit you well and you like and feel comfortable in, whether you are showing, schooling at home, or going trail riding with friends. If you are uncomfortable or getting rubs, you are not going to ride well, and this affects your horse. You have to feel good in what you wear, and it has to help you be athletic if you want the competitive edge that brings out the best in your horse.

POSITIVE INFLUENCERS

– *Laura Cotter* –

I would love to have spent more time with trainer Laura Cotter, but at the time I had another job and only ended up staying with her about six months or so. Blue Bar Farm was, at the time, one of the biggest names in Quarter Horses—it was a great atmosphere. In a short period, I learned so much (including how to foal out mares because my apartment happened to be right near the foaling stalls—I don't think that was a coincidence!). Yes, I learned a lot from Laura, but what really impressed me about her was that at all times and in all places, in and out of the arena, she looked like an equestrian professional. In the barn, at an evening out with clients, at the show…it didn't matter. She dressed and looked the part.

Laura also had a cordiality and manner of talking to people that made them feel welcome and comfortable. She listened and appreciated what you might add to the conversation.

Maybe her most remarkable lesson for me was her sportsmanship. She showed a lot in conformation classes, where she didn't have the element of performing and trying to outdo others and their performances. She was being strictly judged on how her horse was built. She would always, no matter who it was, congratulate the winner. And that was something that really taught me good sportsmanship. The professional that she was, first class all the way, taught me how to keep impeccable records of how I cared for the horses, and also of our show performances.

Laura went on and worked for Wayne Lukas in the racing industry for years. She was an incredibly talented horsewoman. I wish I could have worked with her longer, but she is an example of how people who are only present in your life for a short period of time can be hugely influential.

Even When You're Good, It's Not Always Easy

In 1991, I piloted my third Quarter Horse to a fourth AQHA Superhorse win. This time, it was a son of Rugged Lark, The Lark Ascending (I talk more about him on p. 88), and a very important person had become an integral part of my team.

It was this year that my now-husband Cyril and I started our professional relationship. We came from very different backgrounds but similar equestrian foundations based in French classical dressage. It was our team effort that made it possible to win the title. Cyril was my coach, and I was the competitor. We almost made the Finals in the Trail and Western Riding competitions, but ultimately the Superhorse was won with points in the Hunter Under Saddle, Hunter Hack, Working Hunter, and Pleasure Driving classes. At that time, the competition did not include Performance Halter, where I knew The Lark Ascending would have been a favorite with his balanced athletic conformation, beautiful head, and slender neck that tied perfectly into his shoulder.

Another fun part of the equation were The Lark Ascending's owners—newcomers to the AQHA scene. Sisters Janet Reid and Ethel Strach from Michigan would be the winners of a title they did not know anything about without our guidance! They later became longtime breeders and had two sons of Rugged Lark. It was always fun to work with people new to the business and the enthusiasm and energy they brought, but it was even better when the clients accomplished something most breeders and owners wait a lifetime to do!

Although I won the Superhorse with The Lark Ascending excelling in the hunter classes, honestly, over-fences training and showing was a skill that took a while for me to grasp. I was very inconsistent and could not always find the distance for the correct takeoff. When Cyril and I began working together, I began to get the help I needed, as he specialized in show jumping and had been trained to teach riding during his education at the French National Riding School, the famed Cadre Noir in Saumur. But still, I would defeat myself because I could not easily see the distance.

Later, when I found I had a special horse with talent over fences, I hired Colleen McQuay, Shane George, Bill Ellis, and Lanie DeBoer to show him

5.3 • I competed Rugged Son by Rugged Lark in Hunter Hack and Working Hunter classes. He was a natural: relaxed, balanced, with scope over a jump. I, however, was never a natural over fences. I had to work very hard to find distances and despite the fact I always enjoyed it, winning in that arena was a challenge for me.

5.4 • Cyril and I leading a group of students on a trail ride in Florida. It is our rule we only walk on the way back home—trot or canter on the way out.

in the Working Hunter events. They were experts and it was the only discipline they did. I learned everything I could working with and watching these wonderful horsemen, and eventually was very successful in Hunter Hack and Working Hunter. But still, to date, I believe there are just some who have a natural knack for finding the correct distance that allows the horse to have his best balance and form, and thus the most scope over a fence. I will do dressage fundamentals with my horses, and when it really matters, hand the horse to an expert to compete in the hunters! The competitive standard means knowing when you need help and not being afraid to ask for it—even if you never leave your property.

Ride Smart

Mostly, "competitive standard" just means you "ride smart." You have to ride smart to be on your game in a competitive event, whatever discipline it may be. Consider the different aspects of a competition. For example, you have a warm-up. In the warm-up, you need to know the other riders—the ones to stay away from (they are having trouble with their horses) or the ones you want to beat (get close to that rider). You have to build a strategy for any part of any event in any competition. What you want to do and where. You have to have a plan so you can then use your instincts to work on your behalf in the moment. Let's say my horse tends to increase his speed going toward the gate of the arena. It would be my plan to remind the horse to stay at the same speed in the middle of the short side of the ring and then be ready to remind the horse again when I get him straight on the long side of the ring toward the gate. I would know and plan this before I compete in the event.

The same smartness is even more important for the trail rider, for example, because you don't have the arena to help you establish control. The horse will always be slower going away from home, the trailer, or his stall and a whole lot more enthusiastic to go back! Why do horses do this? It is their herd and "homing" instincts. Herd and home are where they feel safe and confident. For some horses it is more important than others, but you will never change it in a horse. (So, trail riders, if you want to do more than walk when you next go out, trot or canter on your way away from home, and always walk on your way back!)

Reward Your Horse

So many kids, amateurs, and professionals, too—both recreational riders and competitors these days—don't reward the horse. Even just with a soft voice that should always be used in moments of praise (horses should learn to recognize this from the groundwork you do—see p. 31). What gives you a winning style, whether you compete or not? Stopping and giving your horse a pat and some praise—"THAT'S what I wanted! Super job!"

POSITIVE INFLUENCERS

– Colleen McQuay –

As a rider, Colleen McQuay was a six-time Quarter Horse Congress Champion and multiple-time AQHA World Champion. Her students, including her daughter Mandy, were hugely successful as junior riders and in the hunters. I met Colleen when I rode with her husband Tim in the eighties and watched in awe as she would put together a string of 20 horses to go to a horse show and she'd do *everything*: entries, transportation, tack, clothes, feed, bedding, riders, staff…*everything*.

She could orchestrate amazing and unique events on a large scale, and I always traced it back to that example of organizing 20 horses to go to a show. She had a system that translated from one to the other. But it also all came down to her determination and organization. If Colleen decided she was going to make something happen, she did it. I was just a single girl in the cowboy world back then and seeing her determination on the business side of things taught me that with the same skills, I too could be successful.

I say to some riders they should overpraise their horses—praise them more than they would normally because the horses finally understood what they were asking! I don't see enough people praising their horses for good responses, however small. In some areas of the industry now, they drill a movement over and over and over and over, with only correction, and no praise. They just keep riding their horses like nothing has happened, and then when the horse doesn't do something right, they notice and make a thing about it. But when it is correct, smooth, easy, responsive, and willing, they aren't saying, "Yes! GOOD!"—and they should.

Tips for Gaining a Competitive Edge

For the Competitor

★ Walk your test or pattern on foot in the show arena that you are going to compete in. This will help with accuracy and planning what you are going to do and when.

★ Build a strategy to improve aspects of performance from your previous show or class. Keep it simple and achievable.

★ If possible, find a place where you can warm up your horse with as few other people as possible and with good ground for your horse. When a warm-up or show arena is crowded with lots of horses, only walk.

5.5 • Reviewing my Western dressage test with the help of Sherlock, Watson, and Hudson.

★ When you have the opportunity, walk your horse around the show arena in-hand. If your horse is excited, nervous, or worried, find a place to longe him, then go back to the show arena and work him in-hand in both directions of the ring to build his confidence. If your horse is confident, he will work as close as he can to the way he does for you at home.

★ If your horse is worried about a certain spot around or in the arena, spend time there! Practice slow maneuvers—turn-on-the-forehand, yielding, backing, side-pass, standing square on a loose rein. After a maneuver, turn toward the area that is causing the worry (see p. 109). Never "turn tail" to a "scary spot" if the horse is showing anxiety. You will build his confidence by spending time looking at or working near the spot in question. Find a friend and have a visit, with your horses standing near the place of concern as you carry on a great talk. It all goes away for the horse!

★ Don't overschool or drill a horse before competition or training. If he has done something well one time, reward him and go to something else. Always change up what you are doing with horses. They love variety and will keep concentrating for you.

For the Recreational Rider

★ Know the trails or roads you plan to ride on. It is best to go with a friend on an experienced horse if yours is young or inexperienced, in order to build confidence in your horse.

★ I have mentioned this before but it is important, so I'll say it again: When riding in groups, ride with people who know you and your horse and who you know will respect what you need to do to stay confident and safe. Do not ride with groups who make you uncomfortable.

★ When riding on a trail you don't know well, make sure your horse wears a halter under his bridle and that there is a lead rope tied around his neck. This gives you the option to get off and lead him if you run into an area where you feel insecure or unsure. This decision is always okay. Getting off your horse is not letting him "win." There are many situations when you will be safer on the ground. When you and your horse find a spot where you feel confident again, you can remount and go on.

★ Exercise your horse before you go on a trail ride. There is nothing wrong with a light longeing session or a little liberty work before heading away from home.

* Warm yourself up with some upper body and leg stretches before you go out on the trail.

* Wear a helmet!

* Don't look down. Look in front of the horse so you know your terrain before getting there.

My Favorite Exercise for Gaining the Competitive Edge

Work to Improve Yourself, By Yourself—But with Help!

Our friend, benefactor, and client Heidi Burkhalter (see p. 165) was one of the first examples of "remote training," which is so common now. We sold her a wonderful mare, who she took back to her home in Switzerland (I tell you the story on p. 167). The horse was solid, and Heidi was willing, so Cyril and I set up a regular correspondence via phone and fax to gauge her progress and help her prepare for shows on the European Quarter Horse circuit. We would talk to Heidi about what was going on with her horse, what she was seeing on the ground and feeling in the saddle, then fax her lesson plans to follow on her own. Heidi had immense success with this system, despite being an example of someone with the right intentions, the caring for the horse, the desire to do well (all the qualities you'd want to see in a person interested in horse ownership) but very little talent or natural ability.

It is important to have some guidance when working with horses, for reasons of safety more than anything, but the competitive edge can mean having the independence and the level of commitment needed to take a trainer's advice or skills you learn, then apply them on your own in a consistent and correct way. You can try it:

> "I WOULD RATHER REGRET THE THINGS
> I HAVE DONE THAN REGRET
> THE THINGS I HAVE NOT DONE."
>
> – LUCILLE BALL –
> Actress

★ Take a lesson and ask your instructor for three things to work on while on your own in order to continue building toward your goals.

★ Audit a clinic and take notes that you can apply in a sensible way toward the work you are doing with your horse.

★ Try a virtual lesson using PIVO Meet (for example) so you can check in with a knowledgeable trainer on a regular basis about your progress, even if you can't do so in person.

★ Like Heidi, establish a system of correspondence with a trainer that helps provide a framework you can follow on your own with your horse's type, stage of development and training, and your riding goals in mind.

5.6 • Take lessons with the intention of using what you learn to work with your horse on your own. Whatever our age and whatever our goals, we are all building toward a lifetime of enjoying horses.

When you think about creating your own Superhorse from the horse you have in the barn, remember you don't need your hand held to do it. You don't need to be managed every second. You should be enjoying the horse, the experience, and the process—that is what it is really all about.

— CHAPTER 6 —

OPTIMISM AND ETHICS ARE THE KEYS TO SUCCESS

*"It will be alright.
Things will work out okay."*

– Heidi Burkhalter –

IN 1992, I was hired by the Swiss Quarter Horse Association to teach a clinic. Heidi and Walter Burkhalter hosted me at their home in Switzerland, and we hit it off so well, the encounter was the beginning of a lifelong friendship. They were the nicest people and treated me like a queen! (They even put an American flag on their pole at their house, in my honor.) I ended up returning to Switzerland, Germany, and Italy for the next 14 years to teach and show the Quarter Horses that so many there loved. It was so much fun, and a true thrill to compete at the famous Aachen competition grounds.

Over time, the Burkhalters became clients. Heidi was the "horse nut." I would work with her while in Switzerland, but her horse was always difficult for her. His gaits were too rough, he was too sensitive for her skillset, and he was too big for her small self to handle. He just wasn't a good match. She tried several others, but they were too hot, too sensitive, too bouncy. After three or four didn't work out, I knew Heidi's happiness and safety depended on finding the right fit.

Well, I had an Appendix Quarter Horse mare that I had raised that happened to be named Larks Swiss Miss. (I had named her that because I had been skiing in Switzerland when my mom called to tell me that a beautiful bay daughter of Rugged Lark had been foaled.) One year, Heidi came to the Royal Palm Ranch in Michigan with friends, and I had "Swiss" there, as her owner was going to college and needed to sell the mare. Heidi asked if she could ride her, and they got along so well!

"Okay," Heidi said. "I will take Swiss to Switzerland."

Heidi had many fabulous years with Swiss. She drove her, rode her English, and rode her Western. Heidi had me show Swiss in Switzerland and Germany and the mare was soon the top all around horse in Europe. She also won the All-Around Open Horse at the two top Western horse shows in Germany. (And Heidi ended up buying several more horses from me.)

Heidi and Walter (who started riding when he retired at 67) also became wonderful business mentors and benefactors. Our friendship grew quickly: with every visit to Switzerland, I would go to a new ski area with Walter, and a new horse show with Heidi. We really enjoyed each other, and I also got to know their wonderful kids. One of their daughters, Karin, even came to work with me and Cyril for nearly 10 years.

In 1997, Cyril and I were looking for a farm to buy in Ocala, Florida. I found one that we just loved, but it was just a bit more expensive than our budget. I will never forget the day I called Heidi to talk to her about it. I asked her if she would buy the farm and allow Cyril and me to buy it back from her, over time, and in payments.

"Well," she said at first, "Walter is on a sailing trip, and I would like to talk to him about it."

I was incredibly grateful that Heidi was even thinking about my proposal. But then, before we ended the call, she suddenly exclaimed, "Lynn, we will buy the farm!"

Twenty years after that call, we paid for Fox Grove Farm in full, and owned it outright for a long time before selling in 2022 when we chose to downsize our operation. Riders from all over the world joined us at Fox Grove through

6.1 A & B • Larks Swiss Miss was Europe's top all-around Quarter Horse for many years. I persuaded our friend and client Heidi Burkhalter to buy her, and it was a perfect fit. I spent many years traveling to Switzerland to provide training and showing support. "Swiss" was taught to drive, as most of my horses were, and her ability in front of a cart added to her crossover appeal.

6.2 • With my friend and client Heidi Burkhalter as we celebrate Larks Swiss Miss as a Multiyear All-Around Open and Amateur European Champion.

the years. And I know Heidi and Walter were angels from heaven—there is no better reward than to have people trust you, believe in you, and open the doors for you to make your own success.

It was Heidi who taught me the beauty of positivity. In all our time together, I never knew her to get cross or mad about anything. She would always say, "It will be alright," or "I'll try again tomorrow," when things weren't going well. Her optimistic outlook always kept her in a mental state that ensured she could excel at riding even though she wasn't athletically talented. Her expectations weren't unrealistic. There was never pressure from the outside or the inside in her horse life. Her way of dealing with frustration was to say to others, "It will be okay; it will all work

POSITIVE INFLUENCERS

– *Mary & Bob Byers* –

Mary Byers was a great amateur competitor. She and her husband, Bob, showed mostly halter horses as their hobby, although Mary also rode in Western Pleasure and Hunter Under Saddle until these classes got so unnatural and horses who were not being ridden to the AQHA standards were being rewarded.

The Byers were wonderful clients for more than three decades! They trusted me completely, and I had more horses for them than any other owners in my career. We started with She's My Sugar, then Mission Incredible. A Wild and Crazy Guy was such a fun horse, and Bond Daddy, too! Plus, all the others, including Larks Joint Account, Restless Lark, Rugged Son, and My Royal Lark. Mary loved to buy young horses, have me train and show them, and then sell them to forever show homes. Mary and I were a great team. She loved to travel, show, and most of all, have fun! And that we did!

6.3 • Walter and Heidi Burkhalter with Larks Virtuoso and Larks Shania. Over the years, they bought and enjoyed a number of horses from us. They loved the Rugged Lark bloodlines. Cyril and I are so grateful to have had them as clients, mentors, and wonderful friends. I am so glad they could enjoy horses and Fox Grove Farm in their retirement. They were so proud and happy!

out." And life does. As much as we go over those hills and down into those darn valleys, we come back up the other side. And we are okay again.

The Bright Side

Life with horses is full of challenges—anyone in the business can tell you that. But understanding that "things will work out okay," like Heidi always said, can keep you getting up in the morning and going out to the barn, even when the challenges that face you there seem insurmountable. I've had my share of tough days and bad breaks.

Road Trip Gone Wrong

Needless to say, I have traveled thousands of miles with horses in my lifetime. The one trip that I will never forget was coming back from the famous horse show Quarterama, held in Toronto, Canada, over a week every March. For 25 years, it held the honor of being Canada's largest single breed horse show and the second largest AQHA show in North America. (Quarter Horse Congress in Ohio is the largest in North America and the world.)

In 1989, I took four horses to Quarterama on my own without a groom! I showed the horses and also coached a crew of ladies from Australia who came to train with me and compete. It was a successful show, and we had a lot of fun, too.

As I was traveling home, I had my first—and, I hope, *only*—experience of black ice while

---

POSITIVE INFLUENCERS

– Bill Ellis –

Bill Ellis, who we sadly lost in 2022, was a much-respected hunter judge and member of the National Show Hunter Hall of Fame. But long before he reached those achievements, Bill lived with Cyril and me for three years. During our time all together, he became a dear, personal friend. But he also impacted my development as a trainer because he was a wonderful professional to work beside and learn from. Passionate and extremely talented over a fence, he never missed a spot. Bill taught me to always strive for the top and never look back on the challenges. Instead, always keep looking forward. No matter what horse it is, and what his capabilities might be, you bring him along to whatever his "top" might be. And the bumps along the way are just that—bumps. Don't look back at them and get stuck.

trailering horses. At the time, CB radio was the best way to keep me awake while driving alone, and I also felt that if I needed help, the truck drivers I could contact via CB were it. Well, as I flew down the highway at my usual speed, I got a message on the CB: "Hey, driver with the horse trailer! You need to slow down!" They warned me of the dangerous state of the roads, and over the next six hours, we only managed to cover 10 miles. The horses and I were protected by the truckers! Navigating a rig in that kind of weather was a terrifying experience.

As I headed around Chicago on the way to Royal Palm Ranch in the Upper Peninsula of Michigan, the shackle that held the tires on the rear axle broke. I was immobile on a dangerous bypass in a bad area at night. Thank goodness a state trooper stopped to help me, although he was very insistent that I contact a certain tow truck driver and kept emphasizing what a dangerous area we were in. Well, the tow truck he made me call could not tow the truck and trailer, only the trailer…so I watched my trailer as it was wrenched onto the flatbed with four horses in it *in the middle of the night!*

At the repair shop, I pulled my truck up next to the tow truck and trailer and slept fitfully beside it until daybreak when I fed and watered the horses (still in the trailer, still on the tow truck). When the shop opened, I held my breath until I could safely unload all four horses and find a place to put them as the trailer shackle and axle were repaired. Thousands of dollars later in towing expenses and repairs, we were back on the road.

Unbelievably, I later discovered a stable, owned by a professional trainer I knew, was only two miles down the road from where I broke down. The trainer could have picked up me and the horses, and we would not have gone through the nightmare on the side of the interstate. No cell phones at that time, however. And, looking back, I came to feel the trooper was in cahoots with the tow truck driver and repair shop, as he gave me no choice other than to do as he said.

★ *LESSON LEARNED: Don't travel alone without a cell phone—and don't always trust your policeman…*

The Room Next to My Mom's

My first hobby and love is skiing, and I actually met my first husband, Peter Palm, while skiing with friends. We built a house together at the Big Powderhorn ski area in Bessemer, Michigan, where he managed the lodge, but we were looking for property where I could have a boarding and training business because I already had a start in the equine industry when we met. We eventually found what would become Royal Palm Ranch—a great era of 10 years in the Upper Peninsula: 100 acres, with 30 acres already cleared for an abandoned farm. (Just a funny side story: The previous owner had sold topsoil off the farm in exchange for cases of beer; he had the largest pile of beer cans outside his kitchen window that I'd ever seen in my whole life!) The other 70 acres was wooded and a fabulous place to school horses outside the arena. I had one young horse who was weak in the topline, so during the summer I would trot her from our ranch through the woods and along the road, all the way to the top of Powderhorn Mountain, then we'd walk home. I loved using the terrain to build my horses' confidence and experience.

Michigan summers were great; however, you had to train horses before the flies and bugs came out each day. You did not want to ride in the indoor arena, as you were stuck in there at least a few months every winter. I planned my first rides for five in the morning, as it got light in the Upper Peninsula at four and was dark by half past ten at night. I loved it!

There was a stallion that I was training (and retraining); his owner—and supposed trainer—was having trouble. I found the stallion to be so smart that he had basically learned how to "control his people." He was not dangerous...but close to it. As my training career had specialized in working with stallions, I knew how important it was for the horse to respect you and how much you had to be consistent in his handling. I was endlessly working with my farm staff, explaining the need to always handle the horse in the same way with expectations he understood, but it was a challenge. Most people just didn't get the importance of consistency.

6.4 A & B • With Rugged Lark at Royal Palm Ranch in Bessemer, Michigan. We had many happy years with it as our base before relocating to Ocala full-time.

It was a beautiful day, and the stallion was a handful. I was first thinking I had to lower my stirrups, as I had been jumping at the end of the previous day and my plan for the morning was flatwork. Second, I was thinking how fresh and cool it was—silent and beautiful. Third, I was thinking of my dear mom, who was in the hospital after falling in her RV and breaking her pelvis.

Well, as I started to stop to change my stirrup length, that smart-ass stallion spooked so hard left without any warning that it sent me flying! At first, I was happy because I fell feet first; however, I heard a snap when my feet hit the nice footing in the outdoor arena and knew I'd broken my leg. I looked straight ahead to focus because the pain was sharp, and there was a rolled-up hose on the ground…I knew that was what had triggered him to spook. Of course, the stallion had taken off, running with his tail over his back, very proud of what he had done. (In other words, he was not really afraid of that hose!)

I hollered for someone from the barn to come help me, and Marie-Frances Davis, who helped manage our barn at the time, ran to my rescue. (I already had my eyes on her to climb the ladder within our business—see p. 233.) I ended up in the hospital—in the room next to my mom, believe it or not. I had surgery and doctors put plates and screws in both my fractured lower leg bones. Thank goodness both my mother and I healed well.

> ★ LESSON LEARNED: *A horse knows every word you are thinking! When you are working with a horse, you need to focus on the horse and resist distractions. Oh, and I also decided I didn't need to work with spoiled, problem stallions anymore. The stallion in training went home and never made it back to the show ring. When a horse gets his way too often, he can become unsafe. I had started my training career with problem horses but chose then and there to move on.*

Performance Slip-Up

At the beginning of this book, I told you about the truly memorable experience I had when Rugged Lark stood like a rock after I left him alone on the

50-yard line in a massive and packed football stadium during a bridleless performance. Well, there was one time when that same trick, which we pulled off hundreds of times in all different kinds of environments, didn't go so smoothly. We were at the USET Olympic training facility at Gladstone in New Jersey, and our exhibition was to take place in an arena full of jumps. I could sense that with the atmosphere and the surroundings, I needed a chance to take him in and give him one walk pass to familiarize him with the space and the objects in it before we tried to perform. Carol Harris was with us, and I told her, "I really need to get him in there before we do our thing," but with the raking of the ring and the tight schedule between classes, there wasn't time.

Well, just like I sensed might happen, when I asked Lark to stand on his own as I walked away to give Carol the bridle during our performance, he ran right to the gate! I had to think on my feet and adjust my program on the fly in front of a large audience. I couldn't be mad—I knew why he did it, and I knew he needed to walk around that ring in order to feel comfortable.

★ *Lesson Learned: At the end of the day, no matter how well-trained and experienced, a horse is still a horse.*

Integrity

Carol Harris taught me the importance of being honest to clients about their horses in training and conservative when projecting show horse potential. This is not only the right thing to do; it is in the horse's best interests, and it goes hand in hand with the atmosphere of positivity and ethical considerations I want to project.

As a professional horse trainer, you have to consider each horse and what you believe you can do to train him and how long it might take. This way, an owner can decide whether to move forward with the training agreement or not.

As there are no laws to control how people conduct their horse business, I often heard and saw unlikely promises made, costs projected way too low, hurried horses (promises of "30 days and your horse will be 'broke'"), and

horses sold with several commissions paid to professionals who did little more than make a phone call. I wanted to avoid such scenarios, so as my business developed, I created a training and showing policy.

Building an Honest System of Horse Training and Assessment, and Client Interaction

Most horses coming to me for training were young, and the intent was for me to take them to the ring in their first few years of competition. I told my clients that their horses had to come into my training barn for a minimum of one year. I then gave the owner a 30-day first impression of the horse, which included analysis of his conformation (form to function), movement and self-carriage, trainability, and whether all this meant that I thought the horse was worth keeping in training for another 11 months.

After having the horse for three months, I would let the owner know if the horse was likely to do well in the discipline the owner wanted for the horse, and if the horse was not, I would suggest a different path. When ultimately the horse was for an amateur or youth competitor, I had to watch the rider interact with the horse, as well, to determine whether the horse was going to suit his owner. If, by that time, I felt the horse was unlikely to move in a positive direction because of a particular reason, I would explain why and that my recommendation was he should leave my training program.

When the horse was proving himself and I was seeing some good development in his fitness, he was retaining his lessons, he was willing, and the owner agreed to the plan I saw as the best fit for the horse, the next evaluation was at six months. From then through the one-year mark was when I started planning showing projections. I liked to give the owner some places to expose the horse and see how the training at home was "sticking." I always took a horse to one to three shows for training purposes only, not to enter classes. This gave me more knowledge of his trainability and an understanding as to how much the horse trusted me, as well as an idea of what it took for the horse to concentrate and work with me the way he did

6.5 • With Rugged Lark at Bo-Bett Farm in Reddick, Florida, in 1987. I learned so much from Carol Harris, Lark's owner, about being honest in my horse business.

> "YOU CAN'T ALWAYS HAVE
> GOOD DAYS WITH HORSES."
>
> – Carol Harris –

at home. The best part of allowing time for a horse to travel and attend shows just to train is that the horse gains almost a full month of training in a two- or three-day horse show weekend.

When all went well with a horse, I usually planned to actually start showing him sometime around a year's time.

Buying, Selling, Sincerity, and Commissions

To this day, I wish there were laws to regulate the buying and selling of horses—like real estate. Buying and selling horses has always been a small part of my business because the suitability of the horse to rider is so important to me. It is not about making money. I have heard far too many stories from disappointed buyers who discovered after a sale that there was more than one commission on a sale. That is not only dishonest, it is unfair.

When I help someone buy a horse, I ask for a "finder's fee." This 10 to 15 percent commission means I will find a potential horse, negotiate the price, arrange the vetting according to the buyer's wishes, close the sale, and represent the horse. When I am helping someone sell a horse, again I charge 10 to 15 percent, and this means I am responsible for representing the seller, informing prospective buyers all that I know about a horse, and marketing and advertising the sale. I try to get as close to the full listed price as possible for the seller while also ensuring the horse is suitable for the buyer, assisting in any pre-purchase exam, and supplying a bill of sale. I will not "add on" commissions for any reason. With some people, a simple phone call that shares information about a horse or encourages a client to buy results in additional commission. I do not agree with this practice. I feel a commission appoints me the lead on a sale or purchase and I do value it as a huge responsibility.

Honesty and good ethics have brought a lot of horse sales across my desk, and it is the only way to get return business. It has given me long-term clients who have trusted me for years and years—like Heidi and Walter Burkhalter.

"That Thing" About Women and Horses

Most of my clients are and have been women. This is by no means intentional—it just has something to do with "that thing" that happens between women and horses. I think it is our born nature to "take care" of others that attracts women to horses. Horses have unconditional needs and many women want to care for them. Just a simple exposure to a horse can start a lifetime love affair. I also think women tend to be more emotional than men, and horses fill a need for companionship and commitment. They can settle our emotions by just being themselves.

Horses fill a huge need when we are unhappy. They are always there for us—warm, loving, and somehow able to understand our troubles. I often say (as you've heard in this book!), "A horse knows every word we are thinking." I know it applies when we are riding, and it is just as strong when we are on the ground. I know when I hug my horse, he hugs me back. When I cry while with my horse, he stops me somehow. When a horse is suited to his

TRUSTWORTHINESS AND DECENCY IN BUSINESS

Carol Harris was so good to me in my early career. She told me stories of how disappointed she was to do business with this person or that person, then discover a lack of honesty, and how when that was the case, she never did business with them again. I saw her very successful horse breeding operation, and since at that time I was just a youngster, still looking to learn, I felt she had to be doing the right things. She and I traveled many miles together, and during those road trips to shows, I asked her hundreds of questions. She was full of valuable tips when I was struggling with a horse and not making progress, or when a horse had lameness issues. She would say that you can't always have good days with horses! So being honest and telling her how the horses were really doing was always the best choice, whether I was sharing good or bad news.

I also learned good business ethics from my dad, and I will always cherish his words of wisdom and guidance. Do your best, he said, and tell the truth, and be conscientious when projecting what a horse can or can't do, and always communicate with owners and answer their questions. When I don't know an answer, it is then my job to find it out! Satisfying both the horse and the client is Number One in my business.

rider, the rider can beam with confidence. The rider can build her goals by getting more fit, by getting her horse fit, and by developing her horse to do the riding discipline they enjoy together.

Working with horses is, in general, a positive thing: riders set goals and work toward accomplishing them. But in that process, the relationship between horse and human sometimes gets so strong that we might not make smart decisions. I have had many, many people—usually women—who I have met over the years tell me stories about difficulties they are having with their horses or ask me for advice about how they can improve their relationship with their horses.

They proceed to tell me all the excuses they tell themselves as to why they have to "keep trying" or why they "will not give up" in attempts to improve a horse's spoiled unsafe habits or see him through an ailment. Again, here are women trying to "take care of" someone they perceive as "needing" something. When a horse has unsafe, spoiled, manmade habits, I always say, without even seeing the horse, "Do you want to end up in a wheelchair? You may if you keep 'trying.'"

If you have unlimited amounts of money, then perhaps you can keep supporting the veterinarians or farriers who are prescribing a lot of specialty solutions but not improving your horse's condition. I tell people in these scenarios to get another opinion! Vets and farriers are important team members when it comes to horse ownership, but like with your own doctors, you have to educate yourself and be prepared to make your own decisions about what are sensible choices to help your horse and what are not. I use my experience and common sense when making treatment decisions related to horses, and I often get additional opinions before coming to any conclusions. Vets and farriers know how to spend your money real well—I have been through it all!

Facing the Term "Unsuitable"

I believe we all can enjoy horses and they can be a source of so much that's positive and rewarding in our lives…IF they are suited to our personal lifestyle (we shouldn't have a young horse if our personal life does not allow us to work with the horse at least four or five times a week), financial means (horses are an expensive hobby), and our goals with a horse (we shouldn't buy a horse off the track if we want to do reining or ranch riding, for example).

No one can succeed with a horse when the horse is not suited to the rider's goals or personal life. I always recommend people make a three-column list related to their goals and what they would like in a horse: *Necessary; Not So Necessary;* and *Do Not Need*. Let's consider an example:

A rider's goal is to have a horse to trail ride. She has three small kids at home, but her husband will take care of them on weekends. The rider also has some back issues. With all this considered, two riding sessions a week is what this person can consistently give to her horse.

What is *necessary*?

* A horse with experience on the trail.
* A horse with some age—at least 10 years old.
* A stock horse breed, as they tend to be the most docile.
* A horse that is already trained well enough to ride easily with the aids.
* A smooth-gaited horse.
* A horse that is not too big (around 15.2 hands, no taller).
* A horse that is "serviceable sound."
* A horse that loads in a trailer easily.
* A great place to board a horse, or maybe half-lease a horse with a friend.

6.6 • Horses are always there for us. My mare Mocha Dell was with me for 29 years—what she gave to me in experience cannot be measured.

What is *not so necessary*?

* A particular color.
* A particular gender (mare or gelding could be appropriate here).

And what qualifies as *do not need*?

6.6 • I love my horses, as I love my dogs, but I have different mentalities when I am with my Dachshunds Joey (left) and Debbie (right) than when I'm with my horses. Horses are not allowed to climb in my lap!

- ★ A spirited horse.
- ★ A tall horse.
- ★ A horse with hoof or leg issues.
- ★ A territorial horse in the stall or pasture.
- ★ A rough-gaited horse.

I can tell in an instant when a horse is not suitable for someone—I don't even have to see horse and rider together, I know by the stories I am told. But you shouldn't need me to tell you when this is the case. I have two important questions to ask yourself when considering whether your horse is right for you.

❶ *Are You Safe?*

None of us can be confident with horses when we are not safe on the ground and *especially* when we don't feel safe while riding. We all fear falling, as we can get very hurt. But when you are always on the edge with your horse, he will know it, his own frustrations and anxieties will build, he will spook more often…and then it is all over. *We* have to know that maybe the horse we don't feel safe with or on is better suited for someone else—and that he is not right for the rider I described earlier who can only ride twice per week.

Both Cyril and I teach that your Number One Priority with horses is safety. We can't let love, or a feeling of responsibility, jeopardize that safety. Today more and more people think of their horses as their pets, just as they think of their dogs as

POSITIVE INFLUENCERS

– *Shane George* –

Shane George is a hugely successful rider and trainer and has won multiple world championships in Working Hunter and Hunter Hack, as well as two Superhorse titles. He and I rode The Lark Ascending to his title in 1991, and he taught me how important it was to *have fun* showing. After all, if you can't have fun doing it, what the heck are you doing it for? That's what won us the Superhorse title together. We were on the path, we were confident, and we were having fun.

Shane always had a lightness of life. He was so talented and so charismatic; a little bit aloof, though—he didn't seek out the limelight. He didn't want to get wrapped up in the politics or the stress or the drama of competition that so many others seek out.

And when he had enough of showing horses, he started breeding and training rodeo bucking bulls. Now he's having fun again!

their pets. Well, more and more people let their dogs, whatever size they are, jump on them. When that same "pet mentality" is reflected in what they let their horses do, without asking the question, *"Do I feel safe?"* then there is a greater chance that someone could get hurt.

❷ *Are You Having Fun?*

When you are not having fun with your horse and with your riding, there is *no way* you will reach your goals and be successful. Remember, the reason we have horses in our lives is to have fun. When it stops being fun, it is time to carefully consider why that might be the case.

Ask the Questions Often

I always say, *before* you buy a horse and several times during the course of horse ownership, ask yourself these two questions. Here is the rule: If you can't say, "YESSS!" when asked if you feel safe and if you are having fun, then you aren't—so your horse isn't right for you. If you have to think about it, and you think, *Yeah, I think so, most of the time, but*...then the horse isn't right for you.

Every time we get on a horse, we are jeopardizing our own safety. However, if we want to participate in the sport of riding and achieve things, in a harmonious way, the horse has to be suited to our skills, our lifestyle (which means we don't get a young horse if we can't spend five or six days a week with him), and what our goals are (we don't buy a Warmblood if we want to trail ride). If you have to think, wonder, and decide an answer, your horse is presenting challenges that should be carefully considered. Get an evaluation from a professional about the suitability of your horse and the goals you have (watch out that the professional does not just try to sell you a new horse!) Having good guidance from an ethical professional can be just what you need to find success, have fun, and stay safe with your horse.

My Favorite Exercise to Determine a Horse's Suitability

Pros, Cons, and What You Learn

I love to encourage people to make a list of the pros, the cons, and what they might reasonably be able to learn when it comes to managing their horses while being able to answer the three questions we just went over *without hesitation*. After you partner with a horse, you get really blind and you LOVE him...but you still have to ask these questions and find the right answers.

Here is an example of a real-life situation and a sample list—make your own list about your horse after you've read it:

Jenn bought Davos, an off-the-track Quarter Horse, because she wanted a quiet-minded but athletic trail horse. Jenn was an experienced, middle-aged rider but a busy professional who could only ride when time allowed, which was not necessarily on a regular basis. Davos vetted sound and was sane and smooth-gaited when she tried him. He was seven, had received some re-training, was pleasant to handle, and was easy on the eyes. It seemed to Jenn like a really good match.

Almost immediately, however, Davos did not fit the bill: Although a nicely conformed and big-bodied Quarter Horse, Davos was not at all surefooted and had little of the fitness needed to safely navigate the hilly trails Jenn liked to ride on. He also had an extreme fear of dogs, which was discovered only after he bolted one day when a dog came running up alongside them. She also found out he had a buck in him when asked to canter, which only appeared on occasion when riding in the ring, but the infrequency made it harder to pinpoint the cause. A few months into her purchase, had you asked Jenn to answer the two questions, "Are you safe?"

and "Are you having fun?" she certainly would have hesitated before saying "Yes," and might even have said, "No."

For years, however, Jenn kept Davos, doing the kinds of things that we do when we love our horses but run into bumps in the road. She worked on conditioning and groundwork to improve his ability to handle varied terrain and used ground poles to work on his understanding of where his feet were in space. She did lots of lateral work to strengthen and balance his body so he felt more confident when asked to canter. She got him bodywork to identify and clear up any strain or soreness. She exposed him to friendly dogs in controlled situations. She consulted trainers and professionals. And Davos improved in all areas, and Jenn's affection for him and sense of responsibility for his welfare grew because he was part of her "horse family."

But still, if you had asked Jenn to answer those two questions, even after all the work and time she put in, she probably would have said, "No." If she made a list of the "Pros," "Cons," and "Can Learns" for owning Davos, it would have looked something like this:

Pros

- Well-conformed
- Easy to handle
- Good in a herd
- Trailers well
- Good for vet, farrier, bodyworker
- Part of family

Cons

- Not surefooted
- Poorly conditioned for varied terrain
- Bad proprioception (understanding of where his body is in space)
- Afraid of dogs

- Bucks on occasion
- Some evasions under saddle

CAN LEARNS

- Conditioning
- Proprioception (to some degree)
- Fear of dogs (to some degree)
- Bucking/evasions (to some degree)

If you wrote out the list of "Pros," "Cons," and "Can Learns," there were more Cons than Pros—and although some of those Cons could be addressed as Can Learns, the question of his suitability for her situation remained. Her age, the amount of time she had to work with him, and what she wanted to do in their time together made it unlikely that he would ever become the horse she truly needed and wanted.

Ultimately, a serious fall and resulting injury resulted in Davos being given to a good home, and Jenn feeling a profound sense of relief that she no longer had to "make the relationship work." But had she addressed the three questions and created a list of pros and cons earlier, Jenn might have been able to find a more suitable riding partner far sooner.

Remember, you are not giving up or letting your horse down by admitting you don't feel safe and you're not having fun. You are doing a far better thing for both of you.

— CHAPTER 7 —

NEVER FORGET: THEY JUST WANT TO EAT GRASS ALL DAY

-7-

"Horses don't have a choice."

IN 2007, I was named the AQHA Professional Horsewoman of the Year—one of the top awards of the equine industry. Individuals who win are nominated and voted on by their peers. My association with AQHA has been that of a lifetime member, competitor, coach, trainer, judge, ambassador, breeder, and author. My dedication to and belief in the American Quarter Horse and the versatility and ability the breed offers has been a huge part of my career.

But there was a time when I began to feel disillusioned by showing and by what was happening in the Quarter Horse world.

Flattening the Standard

As I've already mentioned, I was always competitive, and my involvement in youth 4-H programs amplified that side of me. But I *really* got into showing when I was 18 years old. That was when I had my first registered

7.1 • I won the Western Horsemanship class at my first recognized AQHA show in 1969 on Sugar Baby Bars.

Quarter Horse and had a goal of going out on my own as a horse professional. Showing Quarter Horses meant I could build a record that listed all my accomplishments at the shows and accrue "points" toward competitive goals, and that was a big deal if you were trying to make a living in the business.

Today, the value of the "point" has gone away, and the successes you may achieve within the AQHA aren't as important because everyone is a winner. There are so many levels, and the World Show isn't "by invitation only" anymore, so there isn't enough incentive for a rider or trainer to truly improve. When I started, if I wanted to move up and compete at higher levels, I had to set and attain a certain standard to do that. That's gone now.

A Change in the "Ideal"

In the later 1990s, there was a change in how horses in AQHA were judged. More and more often, they were rewarded for a low head, sullen and tired expression and way of going, and balance on the forehand. I began to find that the horses that I competed, especially in Hunter Under Saddle (one of my best events) and those being developed for over-fences classes or driving, struggled to find success in the show ring. When my horses were no longer winning, I began to feel so frustrated, as I knew that I was not going to tire my horses out, train their heads down, encourage their balance to be on the forehand, or ride them harshly from the hand. I felt very blessed that I had learned how to train a horse with understanding, time, and patience, and that I knew the correct anatomy of how a horse should carry himself in order be truly athletic.

Feeling so sure of my training foundation gave me strength to leave the competition world that I loved. It was a very difficult time in my career to do such a thing. I had reached the top, but it was harder to stay there, and deciding to leave it was a very confusing and frustrating time for me.

Harsh Methods

During the time when I began to doubt my place in the Quarter Horse show world, I walked and rode around with blinders on. Not really, but I kept to myself and away from the harsh riders in the warm-up rings and the questionable "training" in stalls. By 1999, I could not stand it anymore. It seemed that I was never happy with what I was seeing; I was always complaining about other riders and trainers and how over-schooled the horses were for the trail and reining events…and the poor pleasure horses…I knew I had to leave it all.

SUCCEEDING WITH NONTRADITIONAL BREEDS

MY growth away from showing at AQHA competitions eventually led me to regularly competing in dressage. Thanks to the support of my clients, and especially my husband Cyril, I could move on to a discipline that would make me smile. In the dressage ring, I could be comfortable, and I enjoyed showing a nontraditional breed in the sport.

There were many times my horses were "not forward enough," according to United States Dressage Federation (USDF) standards, and there were certainly judges who just did not appreciate the Quarter Horse. But there were others who supported me. Gary Rockwell, for example, an "O" international judge, loved my presentation of my horses' natural self-carriage and my accurate tests. His approval gave me lots of confidence to continue to compete Quarter Horses. Gary even invited me and a very nice Appendix Quarter Horse/Warmblood cross we called Makua to the USDF judges' conference as a demonstration horse for Training Level. I was so proud and loved every minute of the experience. So did Makua—he was confident and balanced, and I was back in an environment where I could be happy with my training horses for correct performances!

I found that even with a nontraditional breed, you can be competitive when you present the horse in a correct balance and outline, the horse shows willingness, and you ride with accuracy. Even today, I get great satisfaction when I can come home with a championship ribbon from a USDF dressage show with a Quarter Horse!

7.2 • My move away from the AQHA show world allowed me to explore dressage and eventually Western dressage, where correct movement to increase the horse's athleticism is promoted. I love the expression on my face and on Rugged Painted Lark's, working here at Level 1.

7.3 • With Lecanto Raider, my first AQHA World Champion.

WHEN THE NEED TO "WIN" GOES TOO FAR

IN chapter 5 (p. 145), I mentioned that my horse Lecanto Raider was sabotaged at the All American Quarter Horse Congress. It was the first time Congress had the Hunter Under Saddle Futurity, and he was a real Appendix hunter-looking horse (he'd been bred to race) in contrast to the smaller, quick-strided, "bridle-path hack" English horses.

In that inaugural futurity, you had a first "go around," then a second; the two scores were averaged, and the top horses from the two came back. Well, after the first go around, that night, someone applied something to my horse's girth area. The next morning, I was braiding him, and he had his blankets on, and while I was braiding, he was stepping forward a step, and then back a step, and then forward and back again. And I thought to myself, *Okay, well...I could longe you and let you play a bit, because you have some energy. But maybe you are just hot and uncomfortable.* So I took his blankets off. To my horror, I could see blistered swelling all over the girth area.

I immediately notified the show vets, and they applied cold water and ice to try to bring down the swelling in time for me to be in the second go, scheduled a few hours later. When it came time to head to the ring, I walked Lecanto Raider up to the gate with the girth so loose it wasn't touching his skin. We iced the area the whole time and never tightened the girth when I was mounted. We got through our class, and I made sure I lined up first so I would be asked to back up first, because I knew that by the time the judge had made his way down the line, my horse wouldn't be able to stand still any longer. We then had three or four days to try and make the area more comfortable before the final round. Well, my poor horse started to lose all the hair in his girth area. With tests the veterinarians determined a combination of wintergreen, turpentine, and acetone had been applied. It was unbelievable to me that someone had done this to a horse, just for one competition.

The best part of the story is Lecanto Raider and I went in that final round and won the first Hunter Under Saddle Futurity at Quarter Horse Congress. We never found out who did such an awful thing. Back then, we didn't have people watching in the barns or cameras everywhere, like we do now in show stabling. But it was things like this that made me eventually say that show world wasn't for me or my horses.

THE BEST COMPETITORS SHOULD BE TEENS

I always learned from Ms. Steele that great trainers will show the same horses for years and years. A sound and willing horse should be at peak performance from just before 10 years old until his late teens. When in his twenties, he may not be as brilliant as when he was 14, but if he is performing his heart out with his ears forward, you have done your job to allow that horse to enjoy doing something more than grazing all day long.

Lax Drug Rules

Thank goodness when I was very active showing in the seventies, eighties, and early nineties. There were no drugs allowed at AQHA shows. According to the AQHA, the association began drug testing at AQHA-approved shows in 1973, and was among the first, if not *the* first, equine breed association to do so. Their strict limits and zero tolerance taught me to develop my horse to be fit and athletic for what I was asking him to do, rather than relying on therapeutic drugs to make him quieter or not feel soreness. My technique was time and patience. When a horse had an ailment, if hot or cold therapy, liniments, poulticing, or walking could not improve the horse, the horse did not show. It was tough luck…and you worked with your veterinarian and farrier to get the horse better for the next show.

When the early 2000s came along, so did the popularized use of therapeutic drugs, following what had become acceptable in the hunter-jumper world. And with the drugs came the trainers who learned how to use medication to "get the horse in the show ring." Usually, the trainers' goal was not to address an ailment, but to mask it. I witnessed trainers who would not show their horses without a "cocktail" at the right time so they could beat the testing system, when one existed. I could not do it then and would never do it now.

I've told you how when freestyle reining became an event, I wanted to do it. I had a horse and got the training I needed. I loved every moment of putting our reining routine to music.

Then I went to what would be my first and last freestyle reining competition, and when I entered the facility's tack room, I saw a chart on the wall of what medications the horses got and at what time. I was amazed it was right out there for all to see. I was also saddened. And right then and there I lost interest.

Now, 22 years later, reining still has, in my opinion, very lax drug rules, with "permitted" and "conditionally permitted" substances that can be fairly easily abused with a horse that may not be fit to perform but "has no choice." Today, competition in some areas of the horse industry has become just "science," with trainers who are "scientists" with the medications they use and the vets who know how to beat the drug-testing systems and limitations that are in place. There is a lack of respect for the horse all around.

All our most prominent organizations—both national and international—allow the use of medications that ultimately reduce the longevity of the horse's performance. You see it in all the horse sports—the "cocktails" that help horses so they don't feel so stiff or so they feel more sprightly, or more calm. I get it...but I also *don't* get it. When a horse is fit and well-prepared, he shouldn't need drugs to do what you are asking.

I would NEVER show a horse that needed medication to "look better" or "feel better" or help hide his lameness so he appears sound enough to compete. I just feel it is horrible, as the horse has no choice. I also feel it is a way of cheating—when a horse is not in top shape to compete, then he should not!

Those who are serious competitors and serious horse people have to reconcile their reasons for competing with such choices. The horse doesn't care about the belt buckle. I propose we take the money we spend on drugs for our horses and use it to learn how to ride and train better.

HONOR IN THE SHOW RING

One year at the Quarter Horse Congress Hunt Seat Futurity, I was training and showing a horse for the country singer Lynn Anderson. She was a new client for me, and as with all clients, I was striving to win. Lynn had a very nice, big, beautiful, brown, hunter-type mare who was a favorite in the class.

After the first two go-arounds, the mare did very well, and we made the Finals. But then she came up sore. At the time, you could not use therapeutic drugs in the ways you can today (something I am so proud of, as someone who showed at that time). I was, however, a master with hot and cold water, poultices, wrapping, walking, and ground handling to work with any soreness or sourness. I was even willing to try acupuncture, as I knew it would help in some cases.

We did everything we could for this nice mare, and it did not help. I suggested to Lynn Anderson that we scratch her horse, that we should not show her because there was a great future for her beyond this one horse show (although, of course, I knew how important the Hunt Seat Futurity was to many people). Unfortunately, Lynn would not take my advice. She wanted to use medications to get the mare in the class, and I refused. I could not bring myself to do something I did not believe was in the horse's best interests, nor would I jeopardize my professional credibility with the possibility of getting caught with a positive drug test. I opted not to show the horse that day, so Lynn took her away from me.

I was devastated at the time. I eventually got over it; however, it was a hard lesson to be "punished" for looking out for the horse's well-being and standing up for what I believed was right.

Many years later, Lynn Anderson told me that she admired my choice to put the horse first, and we then remained friends until her passing in 2015.

Judging and Committees

In the eighties until the mid-nineties, I was asked to judge a lot. I judged the AQHA World Show three times, the Youth World Show twice, and the Amateur World show three times, and I loved every minute of every one of them. However, I was never asked to judge the All American Quarter Horse Congress, and I couldn't understand why. I became very frustrated, as I was not getting judging jobs that I was qualified to have.

I knew that I could never personally reward the horses that were beginning to win AQHA classes on a consistent basis—not by the rules, but by the trends. As the years went by, it was more and more the case that the judges who were getting jobs were the ones picking horses who were on the forehand in their balance and not moving correctly in their gaits. To keep my AQHA Judge's Card, I had to judge three shows per year, and I found myself writing to show secretaries and asking for judging jobs just to stay qualified and legal. Now with the similarities of Western dressage to all-around, ranch horse, and versatility ranch horse events, I find myself judging more shows again. I also have my USEF "R" license (meaning I'm "Registered" to judge through Level 5 for Western dressage. I did one leg of the United States Dressage Federation (USDF) "L" Education Program and learned so much! The organization has such fantastic instruction in the judge's perspective and how to judge—it is well worth the time and money to complete it.

In addition to my firm stances about judging and the qualities that should be rewarded, I tried to make a difference in what I could see happening in the show world by working with the AQHA Show and Contest Committee, the Abuse Committee, and the AQHA Stewards. I could not make any headway. I also brought dressage to the agenda at every meeting and convention I attended. Finally, after 13 years of effort, I got it approved to recognize Quarter Horses in the sport (AQHA dressage and Western dressage competitors can earn year-end awards and points with their Quarter Horses.) I was finally on my way to promote a positive area

THERE'S NO REST FOR SHOW HORSES

There are plenty of fair and ethical alternatives to drugging a horse for performance, and good horsemen make use of all of them. But let's talk about the most important one: **Don't show. Rest the horse.**

In the show world today, there is no rest for horses, and that is across disciplines. I still remember hearing this back in 1998 from long-time Ocala horseman Mr. Raymond Burr, who sold us Fox Grove Farm. Cyril and I spent the evening with him when he was inducted into the USEF Hall of Fame, as he was not well enough to travel to receive his award (his daughter and wife went in his place), and we talked about the need for downtime for horses who competed. He was such a legend in the equestrian world and a man of great wisdom when it came to horses. Cyril and I were blessed to have the chance to know and learn from him.

of growth where I felt the breed I loved could really flourish.

Riding with Common Sense

I spent many happy years competing in AQHA shows. In fact, for a long time, I enjoyed every minute at the shows and events I attended and participated in around the country. It was a fundamental part of my development as a trainer and a rider. So how could it go so wrong? How can organizations established to promote the beauty and quality of the horse change in ways that result in improper, incorrect, and at times, cruel treatment?

Things go wrong for the horse in human hands, and it all begins with people not riding with common sense. It is our responsibility to know the natural instincts of the horse in order to understand him better. When we understand him better, we are less likely to choose methods of coercion or medication to get him to do something we want. And establishing basic good behaviors results in better performance, without harsh training or drugs.

7.4 • Celebrating success in 2020 with WTR Herestoyourhonor at the AQHA World Show and the first dressage classes in the history of the event.

> **WHEN THE HORSE IS NOT WILLING, HE IS TRYING TO TELL YOU SOMETHING.**

And Don't Forget

Remember, a horse only wants to graze all day long, every day of his life. When we want to accomplish our own goals, we need to do it with respect and understanding. We need to know the anatomy of the horse, how it works, and his natural habits and instincts. These should be fundamental to learning to ride well and correctly.

The horse will teach us. When a horse is not doing what I want, I will always ask myself, "What can I do differently?" based on three fundamentals: the correct, balanced position in the saddle; use of the natural aids to communicate (seat, legs, and hands—and in that order); and controlling the horse's balance through straightness and connection of the horse's outline (the horse in profile, from the position of his poll through the shape of his back). This recipe for success is simple to understand, yet, as we've discussed throughout this book, you have to practice with the horse to achieve it. These fundamentals are a must to build a relationship of understanding and harmony, and I believe that willingness in the horse should be the goal of any riding discipline. When a horse is not willing, he is trying to tell you that you have to do something different.

It All Comes Back to the Horse

One of the last beautiful memories I have of Carol Harris was something she said to me with all wisdom, because she was on her death bed: "Always keep an open line of communication, especially when it is most important to yourself or your life."

Her message had to do with the last performance of Rugged Lark at the AQHA World Show in November of 1997—something I will never forget.

We had five retirement performances planned for Rugged Lark that year. It was a big deal. We went to the Devon Horse Show in Pennsylvania, Equitana USA in Kentucky, the Hampton Classic in New York, Quarter Horse Congress in Ohio, and the AQHA World Show in Oklahoma. The World Show was to be the culmination of all and a truly special farewell to an amazing stallion.

Earlier in the year, the Florida Reining Association reached out to Carol and said they wanted to do a fundraiser with Rugged Lark. Carol came up with the idea of asking legendary reiner Bill Horn to ride Lark and "see if he remembered how to do a sliding stop." (Bill was the National Reining Horse Association's first million-dollar earner.) Bill and I worked with Carol and Lark one afternoon prior to the event. Then, during our performance at the fundraiser, Carol walked out into the arena and said to the announcer, "Hey, can we get Bill Horn out here? Is he in the crowd? Will he get on Rugged Lark and see if he remembers how to do reining?" Of course, the crowd went crazy. It was a great time, the Florida Reining Association raised lots of money, and it was all for the good.

Well, that summer, I let Carol know that I was getting to the point where I wanted to break away on my own or do less with the AQHA show circuit because I was getting so disappointed with what was going on and that era of the organization. Carol saw that this meant she might lose me—at that

time, her main trainer—and she started to back away from our friendly relationship and get a little distant.

As the World Show approached that fall, Carol told me she wanted to do the same act we had done with Bill Horn, but with a different well-known cowboy. I was a little surprised as we hadn't discussed it, but I said I would be happy to work with this trainer and Rugged Lark and help them prepare in any way for the event. She replied the cowboy didn't need my help; he had already told her so.

This was the first time I would experience performing at an event with horses—something I truly loved to do—in a negative light. Carol and I had such a division between us at that point that everything we did—traveling to the event, planning my ride times, caring for Lark—was separate. I had no idea what she had decided for the special performance with the cowboy called from the crowd. All I knew was that the other trainer was going to ride Lark the night before, I was going to ride him the morning of, and the performance (where we both would ride) was at six in the evening.

I went to the arena the night before the scheduled performance to watch the trainer ride Rugged Lark. Cyril was with me, and we watched and waited. The cowboy did nothing but walk the horse while we were there. For an hour. So we left.

When I got to Rugged Lark's stall the next morning, he had his head in the corner, which was quite unusual for him, as he was such a friendly horse and so accustomed to travel and showgrounds. I called out, "Hey, Lark!" as I always did, and he didn't even flicker an ear. I was now concerned and entered his stall, where I immediately saw that his neck had dried sweat all over it. I took his stable sheet off and saw that he still had a saddle sweat mark and girth mark—he hadn't even been brushed or rinsed down after being ridden hard enough to sweat pretty significantly.

Worse, he had spur marks up and down his shoulders.

I was crying and livid at the same time. I cleaned him up properly and instead of a morning ride, as had been planned, I just took him for a walk and gave him hugs and treats and did everything I could to brighten him up.

7.5 • This photograph captures so much—Rugged Lark in the spotlight at his last performance before retiring—the 1997 AQHA World Show. What a special road the two of us traveled together—he as an ambassador for the AQHA as I showcased French classical dressage training for the all-around horse. I am forever thankful.

Carol wasn't talking to me at that point. But when she showed up at the barn I asked her to please look at her horse. She looked right at Rugged Lark's shoulders. She didn't say anything, and I didn't say anything. Then I said, "All I'd like is to have the chance to ride Lark before the performance so I can assure him who is on his back and give him confidence."

Lark and I did our part of the performance that evening, and he was tired, but a good boy. Then, as had been planned, the cowboy got on him and started loping small circles. I could see Lark's ears back, which wasn't like him. I turned to a friend and fellow trainer, who was beside me, and said, "Look at his ears. Something's not right."

The cowboy stopped Lark, and then pulled his bridle off. I watched as the horse pinned his ears and swished his tail, clearly unhappy. Then the guy turned around to ride Lark backward.

At this point Rugged Lark took off at a dead run. The cowboy couldn't do anything but hold on to the horn and the cantle and just try to stay on. They did two and a half laps at a flat gallop, and finally the trainer fell off and Lark stopped.

So then the guy had to lay my horse down in front of everyone to act like he was in charge and it was all part of the act.

Lark was panting with exhaustion. His eyes were closed. The veins were popped out in his head. It was horrible. I was devastated.

This incident was why Carol said what she said to me at the end of her life. If only she had communicated with me, if only she had let me explain that while I wanted to leave the Quarter Horse world, I would still be available to her for good riding and good training, then the whole regretful performance wouldn't have happened. But she had taken my decision to change my career path personally and let being angry and offended overtake the qualities she personified most of the very, very long time we worked together.

Carol had always taught me to respect the horse and to always be honest about decisions with a horse because you have to be realistic about horses and life—you are always projecting and setting goals related to what a horse could do or should do. She taught me that honesty always comes with the best conclusions when aiming to keep a relationship going for a long time.

And I had a 48-year relationship with Carol Harris as her main trainer. I learned so much from her. And I know she shared that last message with me because she didn't want me to make the same kind of mistake.

Respect the horse and know that all he wants to do all day is graze! When we want to accomplish something, we must be patient and understanding of him, his instincts and behaviors, age and knowledge, and fitness. When a horse is not doing what we want, he is trying to tell us something. We are the ones who have to change or make adjustments for the horse to be willing.

My Favorite Exercise That Shows Respect for the Horse

When we think we can just climb a "ladder" of levels and progress according to the passage of time rather than listen to what the horse is telling us, we are not showing him the respect he deserves. We are disregarding the signs he might be giving us that he needs more of a foundation before moving on.

One of the most common examples of this is *yielding*. It is a great suppling and connecting exercise for the horse, but I probably see more people not understanding correct yielding, in both English and Western sports, than anything else. This is because they don't understand *straightness* (see p. 16). In a leg-yield, you get the horse straight—you have both sides working at the same time. You cannot do any kind of lateral work with a curve if you don't know how to leg-yield correctly. Everyone thinks this as so elementary, but the truth is, most of us are doing it wrong.

Once you can do the leg-yield well, *then* you can start your shoulder-fore or shoulder-in, haunches-in, and get your half-pass with the forehand leading just a bit. The lateral movements are so weak at the higher levels of competition, both English and Western, because people just get the score they need to move on without getting the yielding right to begin with. I promise you, get yielding right, and all your other lateral work will fall into place.

We need to learn that it isn't just about "good enough" when training horses. "Good enough" doesn't give you the foundation that is so strong and stable that you can build any discipline on it with success. If you are learning through your skills that something isn't quite right, it is never the wrong decision to slow down and *GO BACK*. If your circle isn't round at 20 meters, there is no way it will be round at 15, 10, or 8. Just because you have already done the 20-meter circle doesn't mean you need to move on to the more challenging figure. It is when that 20-meter circle is correct and round that you *then* move on and try one at 15 meters.

Yielding and circles are fundamental exercises that most riders say are "good enough" and move on, but I can promise you that if you don't settle for "good enough" and instead work to get them right, your stronger foundation will allow you to advance with a more willing, better-performing horse—guaranteed.

You don't move on with horses in order to leave things behind. These fundamental exercises are always there and should always be returned to. One thing that Cyril and I both find so important is that *time is never the question*. We don't train horses to "get it done faster" or "move up the levels more quickly." We go back and start over as often as we need to. If you get your building blocks and foundation as close to 100 percent as you can, then everything else is easy.

The more complex, more challenging expectations we have of horses when competing or performing at higher levels come back to basic, easier things we need to make better. Most people are shocked to find out that the problem they are having with their horse is a very simple thing that $3,000 worth of lessons couldn't fix—it was really just a matter of slowing down and going back to the basics.

Yielding can be done in three ways: on a *diagonal line*, which I explain here, or on a *straight* or *curving line* (I teach all of these in my book *The Rider's Guide to Real Collection*). Yielding teaches the horse to move his front and hind legs together in a forward lateral step. I always teach yielding from the ground before doing it under saddle.

YIELDING ON THE GROUND

When practicing yield to the left from the ground, position yourself at your horse's shoulder on his off- (right) side.

* Open your arms, with your right hand on the halter and left fist positioned on the barrel where your leg would be when riding. (If your horse is sensitive and immediately moves when you touch his barrel, start your touch at his neck and gradually move your fist to his barrel, as if you were brushing or petting his side.) Your right hand at the halter keeps the horse forward and straight at an even speed.

* Walk forward and straight for at least three to five steps.

* Next, bring your horse's head slightly to the right to move him sideways, adding a light steady or pulsating pressure with your left fist. Coordinate your left hand in time with your right hand to ask for the forward-and-straight body position and sideways (diagonal) movement. Do not look at the horse's feet! Look where you want to yield, and at the horse's topline. When you keep your horse's body position straight, the horse will move both sets of legs laterally on a diagonal track.

Be sure you don't control the movement from the halter, which could cause the horse's shoulders to move ahead of his hips. Straightness is the key.

YIELDING UNDER SADDLE

Just as you did on the ground, start by walking forward on a straight line. When your horse's body alignment is straight, ask him to yield on a diagonal line to the right:

7.6 A & B • I am riding Indian Harvest in a leg-yield to the right. To yield to the right, the horse's head should be flexed slightly to the left, as shown here. He is straight and correctly balanced.

* Apply pressure with your left leg to yield his body to the right.

* Use an indirect right rein (the same as a neck rein—do not cross your hand over the crest of your horse's neck) to keep his forehand straight and in line with his hip.

* Support him with your right leg to keep his body straight and maintain even, forward steps.

* Flex his head to the left with an indirect left rein to encourage his forehand to lead the movement.

If you get two or three lateral steps, stop and reward your horse. Give him the opportunity to understand what you're asking and the positive reinforcement to want to try again.

When your horse can yield at the walk from the quarterline to the rail down the length of the arena, increase the slope of the diagonal line—from the centerline to the rail—to get more lateral movement. The straighter you can make your horse, the more he can cross his hind legs as much as his front legs and maximize his lateral step. Take the time to develop this—as I've explained, it is the foundation exercise and you shouldn't have expectations of other skills or moving up levels until your horse excels at it.

— CHAPTER 8 —

OUR HORSES PAY IT FORWARD AND GIVE BACK. WE SHOULD, TOO.

-8-

*"When with your horse,
remind yourself you're lovin' life!"*

A Focus on Education

I had an idea in 2006. It came to fruition in 2007 and was then repeated in 2008 and 2009. It was called Women LUV Horses—a weekend for ladies to talk, shop, dress, think, learn, and share their love for horses.

The inaugural event in 2007 was in North Carolina with legendary barrel racer Martha Josey, dressage Olympian Jane Savoie, 14-time AQHA World Champion Cynthia Cantleberry, and reiner Stacy Westfall. In 2008, we held the event on the West Coast and hosted the Greatest Horsewoman's Contest, as well as barrel racer Sharon Camarillo, one of *Horse & Rider* magazine's "Top 50 Riders of All Time" Sandy Collier, AQHA breeder and judge Margo Ball, and cutting horse trainer Barbra Schulte.

We were home in Ocala in 2009 where we hosted the Gatorland Mustang Makeover and featured cofounder of Parelli Natural Horsemanship Linda Parelli, and Martha Josey and Cynthia Cantleberry once again. Each of

THE REMARKABLE POWER OF HORSES

Becky Dunning and Peggy Kimes started America's Horse Cares, a special fund to support equine-assisted therapies and activities, through the AQHA. I had the distinct pleasure of meeting a young girl named Mary Lisa who benefited from this fund, which we raised money for during our Women LUV Horses events. Mary Lisa rode at the Ocala Florida Therapeutic Riding Center. Mary Lisa, with her helmet and pigtails, sat on Rugged Painted Lark in a Western saddle. I remember how excited she was, as she had never sat in a Western saddle before. I asked Mary Lisa why she loved horses, and she explained to me that horses had helped her go from life in a wheelchair to being able to walk all on her own with leg braces on. It was so amazing that the movement of horses had helped this little girl find happiness and independence. I immediately became a believer in how magical horses are!

these weekend events included shopping, fashion shows, charity events, and riding and training demonstrations with the featured professionals. I feel incredibly lucky to have been surrounded by such talent on every one of these occasions.

Where did the idea for this event spring from? I created it with Marie-Frances after seeing how much interest there was in the female horse-owner public to learn more about horses and themselves. I had done 10 years of equestrian expos in nearly every state at that time, and I had done market research all along the way. I wished to create an educational event that was specifically for the majority of the horse world...women. Marie-Frances helped conceive and put together the three very successful events.

Along with having fun and enjoying time with other women with similar interests, I wanted attendees to have the chance to really learn from some of the profoundly talented females in the industry, across disciplines. Jane Savoie worked her magic as she took what many thought of as "snobby" dressage and made it into achievable training for any discipline. Martha Josey mesmerized the crowd as she explained how taking your time with a barrel horse would always develop the fastest barrel horse. Sandy Collier, the only woman at that time to win the prestigious Snaffle Bit Futurity for working cow horses, demonstrated how you can recognize and develop the athletic horse. Barbra Schulte gave so much clarity to all of us in terms of how to ride and live life with a positive attitude. She was the best! Cynthia Cantleberry, a legend in the Trail division, shared training and show-ring tips to help all riders train with confidence. Stacy Westfall, at that time a young, up-and-coming icon, taught us how to put together freestyle reining patterns to music.

When I left behind training and competing as my main focus in 1997, my business intended to make education primary. Women LUV Horses, to my mind, was a great venue for education about the horse and horsemanship. After our three events, we moved on to new initiatives, but with success and great memories intact.

The Significance of Mentoring

Horsemanship and riding has long been the world of working students and apprenticeships. I would be nowhere, as you now know having read the stories I've shared in these pages, without Ms. Bobbi Steele and Carol Harris...and, of course, so many others. Horsemanship is a craft, an art, and a journey. You never stop learning because horses never stop teaching us, and it makes a whole lot of sense for those who have already experienced many of those lessons to pass along their knowledge to others.

(Some of) My Mentors

I have tried to share a little bit about those who have positively influenced me during my career all throughout this book, but there are a few others I feel I must name specifically when I am talking about mentors.

★ My first big stable teaching job was at a place owned by Andy Moorman (remember her from my story of CB on p. 86?). There I taught dressage basics

8.1 • I enjoyed working with Al Dunning to produce educational clinics for a number of years, showing the places where Western training and dressage techniques can overlap to build a balanced and willing performance horse.

POSITIVE INFLUENCERS

– Al Dunning –

Al Dunning is one of my most favorite cowboys in the equine industry. We started working together at riding clinics, along with his wife Becky, in the mid-seventies. We framed them as "all-around clinics" for developing versatile horses, and I worked with the riders on all the English events.

I appreciate Al's passion for what he does with horses and his passion for good people and being a good person. I would trust him 100 percent with whatever I might need. He is dedicated to the equine industry and to the education of those within it and those joining it. He works hard to inspire people to join and participate. And he respects mentors. (He had his own mentors—I got to meet one of them: Don Dodge was a legendary cutting horse trainer and an AQHA judge for over 40 years.) Al and I have talked a lot about the importance of mentors in the horse industry and feel that is probably the weakest part of the system and the scene today. There are not enough young people coming up under the guidance of mentors who have already discovered what it takes to be successful. It is kind of a dying art. Instead, the trend of the show world—the Western show world, anyway—is to have so many classes and divisions that everyone can go out and win something. It levels the playing field. And if you can win without trying very hard, why would you need to go learn more?

If I was a young one coming up again through the world of show horses, I tell you, I'd be looking around for the riders and competitors with passion, determination, skill, and respect for the horse who I could potentially ride with and learn from.

Al is a wonderful person and great horseman who truly loves horses. I have learned so much from him. He even got me on a cutting horse—a famous one called More Oats Please. I will never forget how much fun that experience was and how hooked I was after riding such a fantastic horse! I just sat there as the horse worked a cow. All I had to do was keep my seat balanced and know where the cow was going to go—something that at the time I had had no experience with. Al taught me a lot there!

8.2 A–C • I love teaching. It is my passion to help others find great happiness with their horses. Here I work with Liz Saylor, first in the arena (finding straightness, then testing it down the centerline), and then outside it over trail obstacles.

to riders of all disciplines. Andy helped me get my first Quarter Horse in approved AQHA shows and she coached me to many awards. She also helped with our 4-H judging teams and enabled me to be part of the champion judging team! She gave me a chance as a young teenager, believed in me, and helped me grow.

★ Dr. Bill Jackson was head of the Florida Extension Service, and he asked me to demonstrate and help teach 4-H programs and clinics. He believed in me and offered an opportunity to share my knowledge. He was a big reason my mother and I developed the largest 4-H club in the state of Florida! The Bowlegged Bunch put on horse shows, judging contests, and the best education programs for local youth for nearly a decade. It was this background that gave me the will to want to be a professional and build a career in the equine industry. Dr. Jackson gave me the strength to reach the top with my horses, and to aspire to the career that I wanted so badly.

★ Tommy and Chris Manion were top professionals in the seventies and eighties with the best horses going, including in the all-around events. They gave me many opportunities to show horses for them. They also asked me to be a guest instructor at their first clinic,

8.3 • A lovely moment on WTR Herestoyourhonor in a Training Level dressage test. In 2010, after years of lobbying for its inclusion, the AQHA began recognizing dressage as a form of competition that "emphasizes longevity by systematically developing the horse and rider to create a harmonious team. It encourages riders to take their time and develop correct horsemanship skills as they progress through each level of training."

which was one of the first for AQHA enthusiasts. I loved to show and win for them, as they were always so appreciative, as were the owners of the horses. We all made a great team! Everyone was honored to work with them, and they gave me opportunities to take my career to a new level.

★ Dave and Sue Page were also top professionals in the business. They had me show or "catch ride" horses for them at all the major circuits. As our relationship grew, Dave was developing a horse named Skip's Sierra Nick with a great owner, Frances Klein. I broke Skip to drive and showed him in Hunter Under

Saddle, Hunter Hack, and Working Hunter. We went on to win my first Superhorse title in 1981. Afterward, we were invited to compete at a USEF-hosted "Versatility Challenge," which was intended to show the true versatility of a horse and was open to all breeds. We showed in Western Pleasure, Trail, Reining, Roadster Driving, and Barrels. We won! And let me tell you, it was so much fun.

* I was hired to coach and groom for Johnny Johnson's two daughters who were showing toward high point awards, and we did what they call a "trailer race" to get the most points in as many events. We showed all over the country and every weekend. The girls would show all weekend; I would take care of them and their horses, then would drive to the next show in the RV as everybody else rested. Today, I look back and don't know how I did it! Johnny Johnson was very difficult to work for as he was a perfectionist, and I had to handle everything to keep the show plan rolling, the horses healthy, and the girls having fun. After my year with them, I went back home confident enough to build an outstanding business as a horse trainer, catch rider, and coach.

* When I worked for Laura Cotter (see p. 152), I met a very unique man named EJ Holub. He managed the breeding operation for Blue Bar Farm. I lived in the apartment in the barn, so I got to know him very well as I helped with the mares and foals. He always encouraged me when I was down, tired, and felt that no one cared about what I was doing. EJ was like a father figure for me. He was a National Football League Hall-of-Famer who played in two Super Bowls as the center for the Kansas City Chiefs. A man of my liking—sports and horses! We built a great friendship, and he taught me to reach for the stars, and that I could do it!

* I worked with popular judge and AQHA President Don Burt on the AQHA Show Committee and the English Subcommittee. We worked closely together on rules. It was an exciting time for AQHA in the seventies and

eighties as they developed new classes. He taught me that when something is right, you need to get the job done, no matter how long it takes. Later he would encourage me to keep trying to get the AQHA to recognize dressage as a worthwhile sport for Quarter Horses. (It took 13 years.)

★ Bill Brewer, one-time Executive Director for AQHA, and I think the longest to hold this title, was the best leader for AQHA. He built such a great customer service experience with AQHA that membership exceeded 250,000, becoming the largest breed membership in the world. Bill encouraged me to get my AQHA Judge's Card. I didn't want a role as a judge to perhaps influence my success in the show ring, but he told me at a lunch I will never forget, "Judging is a way to give back to the industry." That was all I had to hear. I do thank Bill for saying those words. He also taught me to be a great leader, because then both people and horses would always want to work with you.

★ I learned so much from Mr. Louis Gheller, who was then owner and manager of Powderhorn Ski Resort in the Upper Peninsula of Michigan. I loved to go into his office and talk about good business ethics. I had started my sleigh ride business (see p. 77), and Mr. Gheller supported me as he loved that his skiing guests could enjoy sleigh rides as a service. We often rode together to Lake Superior, where we would have dinner at a wonderful restaurant called The Sail Inn. I also cherish the times we spent together at his lake home, which I bought from him when he found out he had terminal cancer and his family did not show an interest. I still have it in his memory. Mr. Gheller taught me to always take care of good people who work for you, and they will be happy making you happy.

(Some of) My Mentees

Because of the belief I have in the importance of equestrian education and sharing knowledge, and because of how thankful I am to have learned from amazing mentors of my own, I have tried to use every opportunity I can to teach others. I appreciate so much about all my students—after all, they are putting themselves out there in order to improve their abilities to do something they love. But there are five individuals who I have to say have been pretty remarkable to work and live with. They all had and still have the will and incentive to do their absolute best in life. And I admire that so much.

* I met Stephanie Lynn when I went to look at a horse that was for sale at her mother's horse facility. I saw Stephanie ride and asked if she wanted to come work for me. (I did not buy the horse, however!) Stephanie was with me for several years and went on to do very well as a professional horse trainer and competitor, as well as a really great youth and amateur coach, and winner of the AQHA Professional Horsewoman of the Year. Well, today she is the Executive Director of the National Snaffle Bit Association! I am so very proud of her, as she has taken the NSBA to exciting new places.

* Kevin Dukes came to one of our equestrian schools at the Royal Palm Ranch in Bessemer, Michigan. He did so well at the one-week school, and I loved his riding and attitude to succeed so much that I asked him to come to work with me. He did for many years, and he was a good enough rider to show horses that I had in training and did an excellent job with them. Kevin went on to build his own business in Texas, and he is still on top in the AQHA show world, specializing in all-around events, as well as coaching many youth and amateur competitors to world titles. I am again so proud. (And I am also going to get him and his clients into Western dressage very very soon....)

* Carla Wennberg came into my life when I got my first job away from home, working for her parents in Southern Pines, North Carolina. She was horse-crazy and such a good young rider with such talent, I let her ride and compete Mocha Dell, who had come with me. (I had a chance to fox hunt Mocha Dell while I was in Southern Pines—I loved every

POSITIVE INFLUENCERS

– *Cyril Pittion-Rossillon* –

When it comes to Cyril Pittion-Rossillon, where do I begin? How we met was meant to be…he came from France to learn about Quarter Horses from Carol Harris. I came from Michigan to the same Bo-Bett Farm to lease a barn to show my horses in the winter. Rugged Lark was one of them. I had just recently completed my divorce from my first husband, and any relationship with a man was the furthest thing from my mind.

When Cyril and I met, we hit it off. He was watching me ride a hunter-type horse that I was training over fences, and when I was done, I asked him if he had any advice for me, as I had heard he was a jumper rider. Two years after that, we were married, and he is still my best friend 33 years later!

Cyril's amazing education from the French National Equestrian School, the famed Cadre Noir, has helped take my desire to educate riders to be well-rounded horsemen to new levels. He is the one who taught me how to develop a lesson plan:

- *Identify the subject of the lesson.*

- *Explain to the student why the subject of the lesson will be taught that day.*

- *Explain the exercises that address the subject of the lesson.*

- *At the end, summarize what you worked on and ask questions to make sure the rider understands the "why" and the reasons for the lesson.*

It was easy for me to learn this because Ms. Steele always taught me the "why." I think that is the responsibility of a horsemanship or riding instructor. When students can understand "why," they will be more likely to practice well and ultimately achieve better skill. Cyril and I share respect and passion for the horse. That is why we will always work very well side by side. He taught me that being best friends is how to keep a relationship lasting. Cyril is a kind man, appreciates women, and is a smart, very talented rider and instructor. From him I learned you can spend the rest of your life with someone, as I know we will until we die.

8.4 • Happy horses and happy riders receiving instruction from Cyril and me. He and I have such a similar foundation of work in dressage fundamentals for English and Western riders, and we have a common goal of setting riders and horses up for success with each other, so they both can perform their best.

minute!) Carla, who has been an AQHA judge for over 30 years and was named AQHA Professional Horsewoman of the Year in 2008, grew up to really love teaching. She has been very involved in the Intercollegiate Horse Shows Association (IHSA) and coached equestrian teams at several colleges (she is currently at St. Andrews University in Scotland County, North Carolina), serving as a mentor for thousands of young riders. The thing that I think makes her truly special is how much she believes in horsemanship education and how she has taken the lessons she learned from me and Mocha Dell all those years ago, and many others since, and is passing them on.

★ In 1985, Paola Donarini Masi came from Italy to meet me at the AQHA World Show in Oklahoma City. She had never been to Oklahoma—nor had she ever met me. She had followed my popularity and success in *The American Quarter Horse Journal* and had reached out, asking to train with me. Well, when Paola reached the show, I was actually in the arena competing in a Trail class with Majestic Signal, a wonderful gelding bred by Carol Harris. I was at the last obstacle, which involved picking up a sack of feed from the top of a barrel and transferring it to another barrel. Paola arrived just in time to see the bag slip from my hand to the ground! I had to get it without dismounting, so I reached down so far my opposite leg was almost over the seat of the saddle. I managed to retrieve the bag and finish the class in first. Believe it or not, I had a second horse in the class who tied Majestic Signal, with the tie breaker ultimately going for him.

Meeting Paola after that class was a very unique way to start our trainer-apprentice relationship! The first horse I put her on was Rugged Lark. She could not even steer him then, but she was very naturally talented and spent the next three years coming on three-month visas to ride with me. I also went to Italy to teach her and her own clients, who were all crazy for Western horses and Western riding. She married a wonderful horseman named Fillipo Masi who brought the sport of reining to Italy while she trained and competed All-Around Horses, and her sons Micki

8.5 • Marie-Frances Davis with DGS Replicated, who started his all-around show career with me in dressage.

and Dido grew up in the business, as well. She has now been a mentor to far more young riders than I have.

★ I met Marie-Frances Davis at a clinic I did at the West Virginia college she was attending. Again, I recognized a very talented rider who had a passion to do well. I talked to the director of the program and learned that Marie-Frances was a straight-A student too. I worked out an arrangement for her to apprentice for our business. But once we had her there for three months, Cyril and I would not let her leave! After the internship, she came on as staff. She was capable of any responsibility we handed her. I left her in charge when I left on a lengthy show circuit—she did fantastic. I put her in charge of staff—she did fantastic. I moved her to do more training with the horses—she did fantastic. We had found a gem

for our growing business. After we moved to Fox Grove Farm in Ocala, Marie-Frances was given a project to train a horse all on her own from the beginning. I found her to be patient and understanding with the process, and her "project horse" became one of our best schoolmasters. Now, after more than 25 years together, she has helped both Cyril and me build our business with her intelligent horse talents, as well as her immense professionalism and smarts. She has seen us all the way through as we have developed our business model from Lynn Palm Quarter Horses, to Palm Partnership Training, to Palm Equestrian Academy. She has brought our business to new levels, now managing Cyril's clinic tours in different regions of the country, as well as a new event concept she and I have developed to promote Western dressage. We call it Winning Ways—it is a multi-day experience that includes a Western dressage show followed by a day of lessons to help participating riders "grow" their scores for future shows. The next two days are a clinic format to share further knowledge to make them better riders in the sport of Western dressage and beyond. Marie-Frances will always be a part of Palm Equestrian Academy. She has shown a loyalty toward both Cyril and me, and toward our horses, dogs, cats, and business that is hard to find in people. I have learned from her to work relentlessly to achieve excellence...or maybe she has learned that from me!

Finding the Dollars to Make a Difference

I am at the stage of my career where I would like to give back in more ways. Given my interests in Western dressage and my belief that dressage fundamentals are at the heart of creating the most willing and versatile horses you can have, I was interested in creating a nonprofit that could give money to those who needed it to further their own riding skills or the training of their horses in the discipline of Western dressage. But after learning how very hard it is to set up a nonprofit and do the fundraising

8.6 • Working with Adelaide Pickett and her horse Hot N Royal has been an amazing case of coaching success! And so rewarding. She is a wonderful example of someone who is always learning and seeking ways to be better for her horse.

POSITIVE INFLUENCERS

– Neide & John Cooley –

Neide and John Cooley have been great mentors for me and Cyril. In their professional lives, they turned a failing business into a successful one, becoming a leader in the industry. That successful business sold and is still a leader in outdoor clothing. Additionally, they are founders of the Western Dressage Association. Neide has a love for Morgans and John is an outdoor adventurist and owner of vintage race cars.

As Cyril and I sought a different direction in our own business, Neide and John helped us strategize and develop the present chapter of Palm Equestrian Academy. Now our goals are to continue to give back to the industry through educational programs, travel with equine enthusiasts around the world, and promote both the traditional dressage and Western dressage disciplines, as well as within the Ranch Horse enthusiast community.

---

necessary to make a difference, I decided it made more sense to partner with a foundation that had already been established. The Dressage Foundation, which was established by USDF Hall-of-Fame Inductee Lowell Boomer in 1989 and whose mission is "to cultivate and provide financial support for the advancement of dressage in the United States," seemed like a natural fit. I contacted them to see if they would adopt a Lynn Palm Western Dressage Fund, and to my absolute pleasure, we established it in 2019. The Fund has awarded many grants for clinics, symposiums, and camps teaching Western dressage. I am very proud to be a part of The Dressage Foundation. It is all about giving back for great reasons to people who have a passion for bettering themselves and their horses.

What Does All This Have to Do with You and Your Horse?

What do education, and mentors, and donations have to do with your own pursuits of happiness in the company of your horse? It is simple, really, and it comes down to a few things.

First, when you are accepting of the educational component of being a horse person, you demonstrate that you understand that with horses, you are always learning. You are never done. I am still learning every single day. The ways that we can learn in this journey are many. We can learn from the horses themselves, from clinics and instructors, and from mentors who play roles large and small in what might be totally unrelated areas of our lives.

Second, when you are willing to see that being part of a horse-human relationship, being part of this industry, isn't just about receiving (knowledge, prizes, satisfaction, the love of a horse) but also giving some of those same things—sharing your knowledge, mentoring others, being a part of groups and clubs and foundations, loving your horse back—well, then you are in a better place to work with horses. You are open to being the one who gives rather than gets, and sometimes, that's what having a horse in your life is all about.

CAMP NICOLET

Camp Nicolet, an all-girls overnight camp based in northern Wisconsin, is a special place to me, as I spent quite a few summers there, developing the riding program while overseeing staff, horses, and campers. (Remember, I trained Lecanto Raider in the Northwoods (see p. 94)! Over time, I became close to the Camp Nicolet owners, Georgi and Jeff Starz, as well as their sons, Jeremy and Christopher. Having been chosen as Christopher's godmother, I am honored to continue to support Camp Nicolet and the Chris Starz Leadership Memorial Fund, which was established to provide youth from all walks of life the opportunity to grow and develop through outdoor challenge programs.

My Favorite Exercises That Give Back to the Horse

In the spirit of giving, giving back to the industry, and giving toward our future, we need to also think of the ways we can give back to the horse. Here are five super easy ways you can create your own Superhorse:

★ TURN HIM OUT. Let him roll and graze.

★ Train "outside the box" (arena).

★ "Read him" before you get on him.

★ Let him stretch down under saddle.

★ Reward him for good behavior!

How to Invite the Stretch

Stretching down not only feels good to the horse, gives him a break from being in a more collected balance, and is important for his development, it is actually a scored movement in dressage tests. I might ask a horse to stretch five or six times in a lesson. You want the horse to stretch his body as long as possible—the lower he can stretch down with his head, the more he will stretch his back and hindquarter muscles. However, for a horse to do this correctly, he has to be connected from back to front and in an uphill balance, so when you loosen the reins, he'll follow the reins downward and stretch down willingly.

As you ask the horse to stretch down, use your legs to encourage him to elongate his stride without increasing his speed, giving him the maximum

8.7 • I am inviting Indian Harvest to stretch by loosening the reins and allowing him to follow the reins downward. Because he is in a correct uphill balance and is connected, back to front, he is doing so willingly.

stretch. Bring him back on the bit slowly to encourage him to connect and round his spine again. Increase your leg pressure as you shorten your reins and bring him back connected and in an uphill balance. Create stretch at walk after trot work and at trot after canter work.

— CONCLUSION —

IN THE END, IT'S REALLY ABOUT WHAT YOU CAN DO ON YOUR OWN TIME WITH YOUR OWN HORSE

*"Not all knowledge is good knowledge.
I'd rather have useful knowledge."*

IN 1991, I showed The Lark Ascending to the Superhorse title. He was the last Superhorse that did both English and Western events. This was an aspect of the competition that I felt truly showed the versatility of the American Quarter Horse. The horses have now become so specialized that I am sure this is the reason that we don't see this kind of crossover between disciplines anymore.

That said, the interest in the "all-around" horse is coming back after 22 years. I feel this is thanks to the ranch riding horses and enthusiasts. These horses move forward in their gaits, and have a correct balance with the head and neck up and poll above the top line, ears forward, and a willing attitude and expression. My mission for the next decade is to keep encouraging the ranch riding enthusiasts to come "play" in the Western dressage arena. When it is discovered that the horses go in the same manner and Western dressage will improve the performance of any Western horse in any other disciplines, everyone will want to do it.

C.1 • In 2010, the World Equestrian Games (WEG) were held at the Kentucky Horse Park in Lexington, Kentucky, and I was invited to provide a Western dressage demonstration. (That's how long I've been promoting it...and I started 13 years before that!) I rode Rugged Painted Lark, and he was a star. Here we are showing a working jog.

In these pages I have shared some stories and a lot of knowledge. I hope you will find that what is here is "useful knowledge." Useful knowledge when it comes to horsemanship is totally using common sense about every facet of the sport. Common sense is knowing what is good and what is bad. My common sense will always tell me to respect the horse. It also tells me that when an athletic endeavor is easy, you are usually doing it right. When you struggle, it means you are not doing something well or you need to be fitter to do it more easily. It is exactly the same for the horse. If the horse is moving correctly, it will be easy for him. If he is struggling, I need to help make it easier for him to perform well and willingly.

Common sense tells me that, when riding, this means keeping the weight of my body still and in the center of the horse's gravity, which is right behind the withers and in the middle of his back. To keep my weight in the center of the horse, I have to find balance by maintaining a correct posture and position. There is, in fact, no sport that you can do well without a correct (balanced) position. This is horsemanship's common sense.

It is my common sense that tells me I have to respect the horse for him to want to perform for me with my communication through the natural use

C.2 • At the 2021 Equitana USA at the Kentucky Horse Park in Lexington, Marie-Frances Davis and I demonstrated the similarities between dressage and Western dressage, performing together in English and Western tack. I am on Rugged Painted Lark and she is on WTR Herestoyourhonor.

of aids (how I "talk" to the horse)—the movement and weight of the seat, soft upper-calf leg aids that avoid squeezing, use of the hand aids that are just the closing and opening of the fingers, never pulling. If I respect him with conscientious use of the aids, I should have a horse that appreciates me and will work together with me as a team.

When a horse is not doing what I would like in any way, he is telling me, "Lynn, how was your position? How did you cue me? What was my position when you asked me to perform the task?" When I go through these check points and change something within myself, I usually get improved responses from my horse. This is good training!

Useful knowledge in horsemanship is thinking smart and understanding how a horse talks to us. As I explained in these pages, the horse's body and gestures allow us to have an idea of what he might be trying to say to us. A horse talks to us through his ears, tail, mouth, eyes, breathing,

and overall body position. First, when a horse trusts you, is confident, understands you, and is happy and willing, his body is relaxed throughout. What the ears, tail, and mouth are doing and how they are moving show the importance of what the horse is telling us. Their movement shows if the horse is anxious, tense, and worried, or if he is confident and accepting of you and the situation. Anyone can learn to see this if you look at the horse and you pay attention.

Useful knowledge is not making excuses for a lack of knowledge and always wanting to learn more than you think you know. I have worked with many riders who have an excuse for the horse and themselves when something is not going the way they want. This is very confusing for a horse, and he loses interest in this rider very easily or becomes frustrated very quickly. Horses love confident riders! When you make excuses instead of using questions to learn more, you will always stay at one level. Wanting to learn from our mistakes is the only way to become smart and successful.

Useful knowledge is all about feeling, and riding is all about feeling. Controlling each part of your body is feeling balanced. Feeling balanced is when you can control your body so it is relaxed and loose, not tight or tense. Riding is about feeling the actions of your hips (seat), and feeling what your legs and arms and hands are doing. Correct riding and communication with your horse is when you feel light, soft, effortless, with no noticeable movement of the legs or hands when cueing the horse. When the horse is balanced and confident, you should feel the horse respond smoothly to your cues in a relaxed manner, with movement in the gaits fluid and easily keeping a tempo. When we get some of these feelings and they are happening more often and for longer periods during your ride, you are building toward a Superhorse. We all have that passion to ride well, and it is those moments we live for—effortless, smooth, harmonious, and wonderful!

Common sense is knowing that any horse, even a Superhorse, would like to just graze all day, 365 days per year...and on the lushest grass!

C.3 • Phils Rugged Dancer was our last homebred. He was our star school horse who passed at 34 years of age. Horses are magical in so many ways. I am grateful to every one of them.

ACKNOWLEDGMENTS

*Rebecca Didier
and the team at Trafalgar Square Books*

have always supported me and my efforts to educate horse owners and riders from all disciplines of the equine world. Thank you for bringing my thoughts to the page and spreading the message of sound training principles for the longevity of the horse.

Marie-Frances Davis

inspired this project with her recap of my fiftieth year as a professional equestrian in 2020. Reliving those milestones, honoring my mentors and mentees, and celebrating special horses and people in my life reminded me of all that I have to be grateful for. I look forward to many more projects and memories with Marie-Frances.

INDEX

Page numbers in *italics* indicate illustrations.

A
- Accuracy, in riding, 120
- Aids
    horse's responsiveness to, 107, 110
    refined use of, 83–84, 128, 134, 206–7, 245
    sequence of, 116–17, 137–38
- All-around horses
    author and, 20, 80, *233*, 243
    competitions for, 3–4, 5, *7*, 83, *166*, 167
    horse's longevity and, 92 training of, 77
- Alotta Hope, *136*
- American Quarter Horse Association (AQHA). *See also* Quarter Horses
    author's involvement in, 193–95, 203–4, 207
    dressage competition in, 196, *205*, *226*, 228
    judging standards, 195, 203–4
    programs of, 220
    rules of, 200–202, 227–28
    Superhorse award, 3–4, 5, *7*
- America's Horse Cares, 220
- Ames, Dean, 86
- Anderson, Lynn, 202
- Anticipation, positive aspects, 50–51
- Arenas
    at competitions and shows, 156–57
    working outside of, 94, *95*, 105–6, *139*, 173
- At liberty. *See* Liberty work
- Attention, of rider, 84

B
- Back, of horse, 43
- Balance, of horse
    in collection, 22
    development of, 32, 40–41, 119, *136*
    importance of, 85, 206–7
    leads and, 67–68, 99–103
    rider control of, 125–26
    straightness and, 16, 125
    uphill, 98–99, 238
- Balance, of rider
    on circles, 24–25
    developing, 47, 119, 128, *136*, 137–38, 244
    position and, 85, 117, *118*
- Ball, Margo, 219
- Barrel racing, 24, 220–21
- "Behind the vertical," *41*, 43
- Bend and bending lines, 17–18, 22, 96–97, 212–15

- Biomechanics, 4
- Bits
    fit and adjustment, 137, 147, 149
    horse's acceptance of, 54–55, 74
    for longeing, 40–43, *43*
- Blanton, Kim and Tom, *62*
- Body language, of horse, 53–57, 246
- Boomer, Lowell, 236
- Breathing, by horse, 109
- Brewer, Bill, 228
- Breyer model horses, *91*
- Bridleless riding
    author's performances, 46, *48–49*, 49, 69, *70*, *93*
    benefits of, 122–23
    foundation for, 47
- Bridles, 55, 150
- Bucking, 61, 187
- Burkhalter, Heidi, *78*, *127*, 159, 165–70, *166*, *168*, *169*
- Burkhalter, Karin, 167
- Burkhalter, Walter, 165, 167, *169*
- Burnout, avoiding, 88–89
- Burr, Raymond, 204
- Burt, Don, 227–28
- Business ethics, 175–79, 180, 228
- Buying horses, 178–79
- Byers, Mary and Bob, 169

C
- Camarillo, Sharon, 219
- Cantleberry, Cynthia, 219, 221
- Caretaking impulse, 179–80
- Center of gravity, 85. *See also* balance entries
- Chancey, Ted, *90*, 92
- Circles
    as essential schooling figure, 17–18, 96, 212
    exercises using, 22–25, 23, 100–103, *102–3*
    in longeing, 36
- Circus performers, 14, 148
- Claudious Bell "CB," 86–87
- Client relationships, 177–79
- Clinics, 147, 160, 225–26
- Clothing, 151
- Coaches. *See* Instructors and teachers
- Colic, 86–87
- Collection, 17, 22, 41

- Collier, Sandy, 92, 219, 221
- Commissions, 178
- Common sense, 95, 181, 204, 244–47
- Communication, by horses, 53–57, 245–47
- Competition. *See also* specific disciplines
    commitment required, 159–60
    competitive standards, 145–54, 193–99, 211–12, 223
    vs. entertainment, *146*, 148
    ethical considerations, 199, 200, 201, 202
    fun of, 185
    judging in, 195, 203–4
    tips for, 156–60
    training role, 177–78
- Conditioning, 4, 25, 35, 38, 78
- Confidence
    of horse, 83–84, 110, 157–58
    of rider, 138–41, 147, 185–86, 247
- Connection, 18, 25, 238
- Contact
    with bit, 74, 103
    of rider's legs, 83–84
- Cooley, Neide and John, 236
- Corrections, timing of, 92
- Cotter, Laura, 152, 227
- Cracker, 67–68
- Crookedness, 16, 40–41, 55, 132, 134. *See also* Straightness
- Cross-training. *See* All-around horses
- Curb chain adjustment, 147, 149
- Cutting horses, 223

D
- Davis, Marie-Frances, 174, 220, 233–35, *233*, 245
- Davos, 187–89
- DeBoer, Lanie, 153
- DGS Replicated, *233*
- Direction changes, 94, 96–97, 104, 119
- Disciplines. *See* All-around horses; specific disciplines
- Distractions, resisting, 174
- "Do nothing" training philosophy, 68–69, 71–74, 115
- Dodge, Don, 223
- Downtime, 71–74, *72*, 95, 204, 238
- Dressage

INDEX

Page numbers in *italics* indicate illustrations.

accuracy in, 120
in AQHA competitions, 195, *205*, *226*, 228
author and, 88, 196, *245*
as foundational training, 4, 124, 153, 154
- The Dressage Foundation, 236
- Drilling, avoiding, 94, 99, 102, 104, 156, 158
- Driving, *39*, 40, 74, *76*, 77–79
- Drug rules, 200
- Dukes, Kevin, 229
- Dunning, Al, *222*, 223
- Dunning, Becky, 220, 223

—E—
- Ears, of horse, 53
- Education. *See* Learning, by riders
- Ellis, Bill, 153, 170
- Emotions, 179–80
- Empathy, for horse, 19–20
- Engagement, 22–25, *23*, 98–99, *134*, 238
- Entertaining, vs. competing, *146*, 148
- Equine-assisted therapy, 89, 220
- Equitation, 125–26. *See also* Rider position
- Ethical considerations, 175–79, 180, 195–202, 228
- Eyes, of horse, 53–54
- Eyes, of rider
  closing, to develop feel, 121, 134
  looking down, 126, 136, 140–41, 159

—F—
- Falling in/out, 16, 24, 33–34, 37, 100–103
- Falls, 138–41, 174, 185, 189
- Fear, 138–41, 187–88
- Feel, developing, 52, 117, 119, 121–22, 247
- Figure eights, 97, 119, 134–35
- Fitness, of horse, 140. *See also* Conditioning
- Fitting and Showmanship classes, 29–31, *30*
- Flight response, 77, 84
- Focus
  of horse, 34
  of rider, 86, 174
- Forehand
  falling onto, 138, 203
  turns on, 108–10, *110*
- Forward-thinking, by horse, 35, *35*, 95, 103–4, 107, *139*
- 4-H programs, 12, 20, 29–31, 148, 225
- Fox Grove Farm, 167–68, 204, 235

- Frontier Town attraction, 81, *82*, 83
- Fun, importance of, 185, 186

—G—
- Gadgets, 117, 149
- George, Shane, 88, 153, 185
- Gheller, Louis, 228
- Girths, adjustment of, 150
- Giving back, 219–21, 228, 235–36, 238
- Golden Hills Academy, 80
- Green, Eleanor, 86
- Grooming, 73
- Ground poles, *135*
- Ground-driving. *See* Long-lining
- Ground-tying, 32, 59–61, *60*
- Groundwork. *See also* Longeing
  author's early lessons in, 29–31
  benefits of, 31–33, 45–46, 56, 73–74, 79
  evaluating horses using, 37, 51–57
  exercises using, 57–63, 213
  in-hand work, 31, 32, 52, 57–59, 157
  handler position in, 32–33, 35–36, 57–59, *58–59*
  liberty work, 32–33, *35*, 52, 61
  long-lining, 38–40, *39*, 74
  trick training, 43–45, *44*
  voice aids in, 34
- Groups, riding in, 138, 158–59

—H—
- Half-pass, *96*
- Halts, straightness in, *62*, 63
- Hands and hand position, 46–47, 74, 77, 126, 134, 137–38
- Harris, Carol
  author's relationship with, 4, 83–85, 180, 207–8, 209–11
  lessons from, 29, 68–69, 115, *117*, 178, 221
- Head position, *40–41*, 41, 117, 138, 195
- "Heavy" horses, 137–38
- Helmets, 159
- Hester, Carl, 24, 47
- Hind legs, engagement of, 43, 98–99, 238
- Hofstetter, Scott, 150
- Holub, EJ, 227
- Honey, 12, *13*, 77
- Horn, Bill, 207

- Horsekeeping practices, 71–72
- Horsemanship, 6, 57, 230, 244
- Horses
  ambition to eat grass, 193, 206, 211
  evaluation of, 32, 37, 51–57, 77, 238
  relationship-building with, 19–20, 68–69, 71–74, 115, 181, 187–89
  suitability to rider, 138, 140, 165, 167, 177–79, 181–89
  types of, 38
  understanding of people, 174, 179–80
- Hot N Royal, *21*, *121*, *234*
- Hunter classes, 153–54, 184
- Hunter Under Saddle Futurity, 145, 200, 202
- Hyer, William, 14

—I—
- "In front of the leg," 104
- "In front of the vertical," *41*
- Indian Harvest, *214*, *237*
- Individuality, of horse, 63, 89
- In-hand work, 31, 32, 52, 57–59, 157
- Insecure horses. *See* Sensitive horses
- Inside/outside, on bending lines, 18, 23–24
- Instructors and teachers, 20, 159–60, *224–25*, 230, *231*. *See also* Learning, by riders
- Integrity, 175–79

—J—
- Jackson, Bill, 225
- Jenn (horse suitability case study), 187–89
- Johnson, Johnny, 227
- Jolena Lark, *117*
- Josey, Martha, 24, 219, 220–21
- Judging, 195, 203–4, 228
- Jumping, 89, 153–54, *154*, 185

—K—
- Klein, Frances, 226–27

—L—
- Lameness, 202
- Larks Shania, *169*
- Larks Sweet Judy, *58–59*
- Larks Swiss Miss, *78*, *166*, 167, *168*
- Larks Virtuoso, *169*
- Lateral movements, 32, 97, 99, 108–9, 211–12

INDEX

Page numbers in *italics* indicate illustrations.

- Lateral suppleness, 94, 98
- "Lazy" horses, 103–4, 107
- Leading, 32, *33*, 57–59, *58–59*, 158
- Leads and lead changes, 35, 67–68, 88, 99–103, *101–2*, 120
- Leaning, by rider, 126
- Learning, by horses, 50–51. *See also* Training
- Learning, by riders. *See also* Mentors and mentoring
  - author's focus on, 219–21
  - clinics, 147, 160, 225–26
  - commitment to, 6, 25, 236
  - lessons, 47, 121, *122–23*, 128, 159–60, *161*
  - resources for, 20–21, 159–60, 186
- Lecanto Raider, 145, *198*, 199
- Leg aids, 17, 116–17, 123, 134
- Leg position, 126
- Leg-yield exercises, 211–15, *214*
- Lewis, Bobby, 92
- Liberty work, 32–33, 35, *35*, 52, 61
- *LIFE Magazine*, Bobbi Steele feature, 14, *14*
- Lightness, 51, 125
- Listening, to horse, 95
- Longe lessons, for riders, 47, 121, *122–23*, 128
- Longeing, 35–38, *35–37*, 40–43, 52, 61–63, 157
- Longevity, training for, 40, 79–81, 92–98, 200
- Longitudinal suppleness, 94
- Long-lining, 38–40, *39*, 74
- Looking down, 126, 136, 140–41, 159
- Love, for horses, 179, 186, 187–89
- Lukas, Wayne, 152
- Lynn, Stephanie, 229
- Lynn Palm Western Dressage Fund, 236

M

- Majestic Signal, 232
- Makua, 196
- Manion, Tommy and Chris, 225–26
- Manners, 32, 38, 46, 57–59, 184, 185–86
- Mary Lisa (therapeutic riding student), 220
- Masi, Paola Donarini and Fillipo, 232
- McQuay, Colleen, 153, 156
- McQuay, Tim, 124
- Mentors and mentoring, 12, 14, 221–35
- Mink oil, 150
- Mistakes, 51, 71, 138, 247
- Mocha Dell, 31, 79–81, *82*, 183, 229

- Moorman, Andrea "Andy," 85–86, 221, 225
- More Oats Please, 223
- Motivation, of horse, 44–45, 193, 206, 211
- Mouth, of horse, 46–47, 53–54
- Movement, of horse, 4, 32
- Movements, training of, 50
- My Royal Lark "Wills," *33*, *60*, *72*, *92*, *96*

N

- National Snaffle Bit Association, 229
- Nic Nack, 17–19, *19*

O

- Obedience. *See* Manners
- Olsen, Mr. (instructor), 80–81
- "On the vertical," *40*, 43, 117
- Optimism, 168–70
- "Outside the box" riding locations, 94, *95*, 105–6, *139*, 173
- Outside/inside, on bending lines, 18, 23–24

P

- Page, Dave and Sue, 226–27
- Palm Equestrian Academy, 235
- Parelli, Linda, 219
- Patience, in training, 67–69, 80, 83–89
- Pet mentality, 184, 185–86
- Phils Rugged Dancer, *246*
- Pickett, Adelaide, *234*
- Pittion-Rossillon, Cyril, 45, 153, 196, 230, *231*
- Positive reinforcement, 44
- Positivity, 168–70, 175–79
- Professional Horsewoman of the Year award, 193
- Professionalism, 175–79, 180, 194–95, 228

Q

- Quarter Horses, 3, 80, 165–67, 243. *See also* American Quarter Horse Association (AQHA)

R

- Ranch riding competitions, *3*, *151*, 243
- Reactive horses. *See* Spooky horses
- "Reading" horses, 51–57, 77, 238
- Recreational riding, 158–59
- Reid, Janet, 4, 153

- Rein aids, 17, 46–47, 116–17, 123, 134, 138
- Reining, 86, 124, 201, 207, 232
- Relaxation, 32, 51, 53–57, 98, 247
- Repetition, vs. drilling, 94
- Resistance, as message from horse, 51, 211, 245
- Respect, 58, 148, 151, 173, 211, 244
- Rest. *See* Downtime
- Rewards, 32, 44–45, 155–56
- "Ride smart," 138–41, 154–55
- Rider position
  - balance and, 24, 85, 117, 119, 132, 134
  - development of, 95, 125–26, 128–36, 206–7, 244
  - self-assessments for, 56, 121–22, 134–35
  - trouble-shooting, 126–27
- *The Rider's Guide to Real Collection* (Palm), 97, 212
- Riding
  - commitment required, 14, 94, 115, 159–60
  - frequency of, 128
  - fundamentals of, 206–7
  - groundwork for, 57
  - horse's suitability in, 138, 140, 165, 167, 177–79, 181–89
  - preparing young horses for, 38–40, *39*
- Rockwell, Gary, 196
- Round pens, 33
- Royal Palm Ranch, 77–78, 173
- Rugged Cash, 83–85
- Rugged Lark, *176*
  - as celebrity, 49, *49*
  - exhibition performances, 46, *48–49*, *70*, 174–75, 207–11, *208*
  - as sire, 87, *117*, 167, *169*
  - Superhorse award, 3–4, *4*, *7*, 69
  - training of, 45, 68–69, 115
- Rugged Painted Lark "Bruce"
  - exhibition performances, *93*, 244, 245
  - training of, 120, *197*
  - versatility of, *90–91*, 92, 105–6
- Rugged Ranger, *127*
- Rugged Son, *154*
- Runaway horses, 77

S

- Saddle fitting, 149–50
- Safety considerations, 138–41, 150,

INDEX

Page numbers in *italics* indicate illustrations.

170–71, 182–89
- Savoie, Jane, 120, 219, 220
- Saylor, Liz, *224–25*
- Schulte, Barbara, 219, 221
- Seat, of rider, 24, 47, 116–17, 123, 126, 128
- Self-carriage, 16, 25, 32, *36*, 37
- Selling horses, 178–79
- Sensitive horses, 83–85, 107, 109–10, 157–58
- Serpentines, 97
- Showmanship classes, 29–31, *30*
- Shying, 107, 109–10, 157–58
- Sidedness. *See* Crookedness
- Side-pulls, *39*, 55
- Side-reins, 40–43, *43*
- Skiing, 173
- Skip's Sierra Nick, 4, 5, 226–27
- Sleigh rides, 77–78, 228
- Slowing down, 68–69, 88–89, 212
- Snaffle Bit Futurity, 221
- Spanish Riding School, 45
- Spoiled horses, 181, 184, 185–86
- Spooky horses, 83–85, 107, 109–10, 157–58, 174
- Sportsmanship, 152
- Stallions, working with, 74, 173–74
- Stalls and stabling, 71–72
- Standing square, 59–61, *60*, *62*, 63
- Standing still, 110
- Steele, Bobbi
  lessons from, 38, 50, 67, 74, 122–23, 200
  as mentor, 12, 221
  as trainer and performer, *14–15*, 148
- Stiffness, of rider, 127
- Stirrups, riding without, 121, 128
- Strach, Ethel, 4, 153
- Straight lines, 16, 37, 96–97, 212–15
- Straightness
  in collection, 22
  on curved lines, 17–18
  development of, 40–41
  in driving, 74, 77
  groundwork for, 33–34, 40, 60
  importance of, 16, 125, 211
- Streigel, Teresa, 3–4
- Strengthening, 32, 35
- Stretching down, *237*, 238
- Sugar, 12, *13*, 77
- Sugar Baby Bars, *194*
- Suitability

of attire, *151*
of horse for discipline, 38, 88–89, 177
of horse to rider, 138, 140, 165, 167, 177–79, 181–89
- Sun Gold Ray, *30*
- Superhorse
  AQHA award, 3–4, *5*, *7*
  as concept, 4, 20, 80, 160
- Suppleness, 94, 98, *102*, 103, 119
- Sweeney, Bill, 111

—T—
- Tack, fit and adjustment of, 147, 149–51
- Tail, in equine communication, 53–54
- Tempo, balance as foundation of, 25
- Tension, 51, 53–57
- The Lark Ascending "Larkie," 4, 5, 45, 88–89, 153, 185, 243
- Therapeutic drugs, 200–201, 202
- Therapeutic riding, 89, 220
- "Thinking in front of the horse," 140–41
- Thomas, Gene, 86–87, 111
- Tightness, 51
- Timing, 44–45, 116–17, 119, 121–22
- Trail classes and obstacles, 88, *139*, *225*, 232. *See also* Training course exercises
- Trail riding, 73, *75*, 104, 155, *155*, 158–59
- Trailering, 170–71
- Trainers. *See also* Instructors and teachers
  career development, 85–86, 194–95
  working with, 159–60
- Training
  consistency in, 173
  guiding principles, 117, 126, 177–79
  locations for, 50–51
  resources for, 159–60
  school figures in, 96, 119
  session structure, 98–99, 104
  time and patience required for, 67–69, 73, 88–89, 182, 212
  trouble-shooting, 52, 99–107
  variety in, 3, 40, 43–44, 78, 92–95
- Training course exercises, 128–36, *129*, *131*, *133*
- Transitions
  balance in, 25
  benefits of, 22, 94, 98–99, 104, 119, 137–38
  straightness in, 16
- Travel, 170–71

- Treats, 44
- Trick riding, 81, *82*
- Trick training, 43–45, *44*
- Trust
  development of, 40, 46, 69
  in horse and rider relationships, 31, 77, 81, 83, 85
  between people, 168, 179, 180
- Turn-on-the-forehand, 108–10, *110*
- Turnout (presentation), 151
- Turnout, as downtime, 71–72, *72*, 95, 238

—U—
- United States Dressage Federation (USDF), 196, 203
- Uphill balance, 98–99, 238
- "Useful knowledge," 244–47

—V—
- Videos, as tool for riders, 56, 72, 121–22, 134–35
- Voice aids, 32, 34, 35–36
- Voltes, 97

—W—
- Warm-up, 98, 154–55, 156, 158, 159
- Water obstacles, *139*
- Weaning, 79–80
- Weight, in rider balance, 24
- Well-being, of horse, 87, 195–202, 206–11, 238
- Wennberg, Carla, 229, 232
- Western dressage, 4, *197*, 235–36, *244*, *245*
- Westfall, Stacy, 219, 221
- Whatabout Lark "Bob," *95*, *135*
- Whips and whip handling, 32, *35*, *37*, 59
- Winning Ways program, 235
- Women, and horses, 179–80
- Women LUV Horses events, 219–21
- World Equestrian Games, 47, *244*
- WTR Herestoyourhonor "Allie," *118*, 205, *226*, *245*

—Y—
- Yielding exercises, 211–15
- Young horses
  requirements of, 71–72
  training of, 31, 38, *39*, 40, *43*, 182, 186